A WORLD BANK STUDY

Quantitative Analysis of Road Transport Agreements (QuARTA)

Charles Kunaka, Virginia Tanase, Pierre Latrille, and Peter Krausz

THE WORLD BANK
Washington, D.C.

Contents

Maps

Tables

Acknowledgments

This study report was prepared by a team comprised of Charles Kunaka (co-TTL, PRMTR), Virginia Tanase (co-TTL, TWITR), Pierre Latrille (World Trade Organization), and Peter Krausz (Consultant). Henrik Burda (Consultant) compiled the initial database of agreements on which the study was based. The study took inspiration from similar work on Bilateral Air Services Agreements by the World Trade Organization.

The authors are grateful to several colleagues and partners for the valuable feedback they provided at various stages of the study process: Sebastian Saez and Monica Alina Mustra (both PRMTR) contributed to the development of the analytical concept; Jan Medved (CESMAD Bohemia, the Czech Republic), Benham Faramarzian (ICCIMTIR, the Islamic Republic of Iran), Theodor L. Kaplan (KAZATO, Kazakhstan), Anna Gawlik (ZMPD, Poland), and Radu Dinescu (UNTRR, Romania) helped refine the study methodology; Tugba Gurcanlar (AFTFW), Natasha Ward (USAID—Trade Hub), Vijay Tata (LEG-PS), Nora Dihel (AFTPM), and Gael Raballand (MNSPS) provided comments at concept stage; Nora Weisskopf (TWITR) and Irina Trukhan (ECSTR) reviewed an early draft of the report; Gael Raballand (MNSPS), Tomas Serebrisky (Inter-American Development Bank), Graham Smith (Consultant), Rajesh Rohatgi (SASDT), Olivier Hartmann (PRMTR), and Jean-Noel Guillossou (SSATP) provided peer review comments.

Cynthia Abidin-Saurman, Shienny Lie, and Amir Fouad (all PRMTR) supported the team throughout the study, and Julia Oliver (PRMTR) helped improve the final draft. The draft was edited by Michael Alwan (Consultant).

The work benefitted from the guidance and support of Mona Haddad (Sector Manager, PRMTR) and Marc Juhel (Sector Manager, TWITR).

The usual disclaimers apply.

About the Authors

Charles Kunaka is a Senior Trade Specialist in the International Trade Department of the World Bank. He works on trade facilitation and logistics and supports World Bank teams in implementing trade and transport facilitation projects. Charles is about to publish a trade corridor management toolkit and is currently developing an analytical framework for logistics in lagging regions. Charles has a background in transport economics and policy and previously worked for the Sub-Saharan Africa Transport Policy Program and the Southern African Development Community.

Virginia Tanase is a Senior Transport Specialist in the Transport Anchor of the World Bank. She supports project teams across the Bank providing advice on transit systems, logistics and road transport services, as well as on inland transport norms and standards. Before joining the World Bank Virginia worked in the Romanian Ministry of Transportation and in international organizations, including United Nations Agencies, acquiring extensive experience in negotiating and implementing international legal instruments, as well as in elaborating transport policies.

Pierre Latrille is a French national presently serving as counsellor at the Trade Policy Review Division of the WTO. Pierre holds degrees in law, political sciences, and public administration. He has previously been in charge of international relations at the shipping directorate of the French Transport Ministry, served as deputy permanent representative of France to the GATT and then WTO, worked in the Africa section of the Trade Directorate of the French Finance and Trade ministry, and served as counsellor at the Trade in services division of the WTO, in charge of transport. Pierre together with Antonia Carzaniga developed the groundbreaking QUASAR database and methodology on bilateral air services agreements from which the present study took inspiration.

Peter Krausz is a freelance consultant engaged in international transport facilitation projects and research. He holds a pre-bologna doctorate degree in Transport Economics. Peter has extensive experience in transport policy, operations and regulation. He previously worked for Hungarian Railways, the Hungarian Ministry of Transport and Communications; the Budapest-based Transport

Research Institute; the International Road Transport Company "Hungarocamion"; the Transport Division of the United Nations Economic Commission for Europe, Geneva; and TNT Logistics Hungary. More recently Peter was in charge of facilitating road freight transport at the International Road Transport Union (IRU), Geneva. Peter is the author of several publications on transport policy.

Abbreviations

ADR	International Carriage of Dangerous Goods by Road
AETR	Agreement Concerning the Work of Crews of Vehicles engaged in International Road Transport
ALADI	Latin American Integration Association
ASAs	Air services agreements
ATP	Agreement on the International Carriage of Perishable Foodstuffs and on the Special Equipment to be used for such Carriage
BSEC	Black Sea Economic Cooperation
CBTA	Cross-Border Transport Agreement
CIS	Commonwealth of Independent States
CMR	Convention on the Contract for the International Carriage of Goods by Road
CPs	Contracting parties
ECMT	European Conference of Ministers of Transport
EU	European Union
GATS	General Agreement on Trade in Services
GATT	General Agreement on Tariffs and Trade
GDP	Gross domestic product
ITF	International Transport Forum
JC	Joint committee
MFN	Most favored nation
MoU	Memorandum of Understanding
NT	National treatment
OECD	Organization for Economic Co-operation and Development
QUASAR	Quantitative Air Services Agreement Review

ROLA	Truck-on-train, road-rail-road (combined road-rail transport technology)
RORO	Roll-on/roll-off (ships designed to carry wheeled cargo)
SACU	Southern African Customs Union
SADC	Southern African Development Community
SATCC	Southern African Transport and Communications Commission
SECI	South-East European Cooperation Initiative
TIR	International Road Transport Convention
UNECE	United Nations Economic Commission for Europe
VAT	Value-added tax
WCO	World Customs Organization
WEF	World Economic Forum
WTO	World Trade Organization

Executive Summary

Road freight transport is indispensable to international economic cooperation and foreign trade. Across all continents, it is commonly used for short and medium distances and in long-distance haulage when minimizing time is important. In all instances governments play a critical role in ensuring the competitive advantage of private sector operators. Countries often have many opportunities to minimize the physical or administrative barriers that increase costs, take measures to enhance the attractiveness and competitiveness of road transport, or generally nurture the integral role of international road freight transport in the global trade logistics industry.

In the absence of full liberalization of road transport services, bilateral arrangements between countries are preferred. While full liberalization of markets would be ideal, in practical terms, bilateral agreements between countries are the key instrument used to govern and regulate international road transport services. In particular, bilateral agreements play a major regulatory role in cases where no efficient multilateral agreement or system is in place. These agreements vary in scope and depth, but the details they include often reflect the market openness for road transport services between the countries concerned. However, there has not been a systematic way of analyzing bilateral agreements. The present study seeks to fill this gap by employing a consistent methodology to identifying the defining characteristics of regional road transport agreements and the implications they may have on market integration. The study's results are intended to guide countries in their efforts to reform their road transport sectors.

The main findings of the study are presented in two parts. The first part identifies general patterns about bilateral agreements on road freight transport and how they work in practice, followed by a second part which contains specific recommendations on identifying the most appropriate content and coverage of bilateral agreements. The main patterns and recommendations are summarized below.

General Findings

- **The diversity of agreements complicates compliance with regulations by transport operators.** Although various bilateral agreements on road transport may regulate the same sector, each one is different. Agreements often reflect political, economic, or other factors that are unique to the two countries involved. Even agreements concluded between one country and any other two countries can vary dramatically. Freight transport companies often have to adapt to multiple requirements along a single transportation route. This diversity makes it difficult for trucking service providers to comply and may compromise their ability to optimize their operations and minimize costs.

- **There is no overarching international template for bilateral road transport agreements.** One of the reasons for the variation in quality among bilateral agreements is the absence of a widely applicable international template. Bilateral agreements often reflect specific, parochial needs—for example, a desire to improve the political climate between countries—and do not always have a primary focus on improving transport efficiency. Unfortunately, the reasons for negotiating the agreements are not always explicit, especially when they lie outside the transport arena. A major risk is that the content and scope of these locally specific agreements could distract from efforts at regional integration.

- **Model agreements have been tried, but in general their objectives and limitations are not clearly defined.** Regional model agreements have been used in an attempt to lay the groundwork for eventual convergence and integration in regional road freight transport markets, but in general existing models work better between partners with similar conditions. In addition, the limitations of the models are often replicated in the bilateral agreements based on them. In order to be useful and progressive, model agreements should serve as a minimum framework that pairs of countries would be expected to exceed in their bilateral negotiations.

- **The texts of bilateral road transport agreements remain for the most part unknown to their intended users.** Although bilateral agreements should be "public goods" and published widely, governments often do not make them available. This inhibits freight transport companies and other service providers from understanding and complying with the rules they must follow.

- **It is hard to know whether bilateral agreements, once concluded, are implemented.** An agreement between any two parties is only as good as the extent to which it is put in practice. Concluding a bilateral agreement is a positive step, but effective implementation and enforcement are crucial for trade and transport facilitation.

Specific Recommendations

When embarking on bilateral agreements, countries' national and international interests would be best served by taking the following actions:

- Start negotiation of bilateral agreements only when all stakeholders have agreed on the broad objectives and limitations of the agreements. Normally, when negotiating bilateral (and multilateral) agreements, each party's objectives will be to promote and facilitate trade with the other country (or countries) concerned, and to create open and efficient markets, while also ensuring fair representation and promotion of its national interest. It is thus essential that all stakeholders endorse the hierarchy of national objectives and concerns that negotiators should have in mind. The stakeholders should also agree on the linkage between specific provisions of the agreement and the achievement of those objectives. Such endorsement would also ensure the basis for effective implementation of the agreement once it is enacted.

- Include core elements in any bilateral road transport agreement. The core elements cover and regulate the most important aspects of the transport operation. These should include, for example, scope, permit management, transit rights, routes, and cabotage and other limitations. These core elements limit the possibilities of misinterpretation, rent-seeking behaviors, and other inefficient practices. Core elements also provide a "standardized" basis for assessing and comparing individual agreements. When bilateral agreements contain these core elements, they can be an effective indicator of the degree of openness of the road transport markets between countries. An index of openness can, in turn, provide a basis for technical assistance during negotiations of agreements and reform processes that may follow. The present study lays a foundation for the eventual development of an index of openness of road transport markets.

- Emphasize qualitative over quantitative and multilateral over bilateral regulation. Worldwide experience has proven that when strictly and properly implemented, the international qualitative regulation of market access leads to more competition, particularly in freight transport markets. Qualitative regulation may include forward-looking requirements for access to the profession, road safety rules, security, protection of the environment, and so forth. Such qualitative standards are preferable to quantitative restrictions of market access. Among the results can be better delivery scheduling, which leads to improved international logistics and supply chains and improved trade and international production schemes. Good qualitative regulation can also lead to enhanced freight rate competitiveness, leading to reduced transport costs.

- Adopt the principle of freedoms. Any effective qualitative regulatory scheme should be underpinned by internationally accepted principles of free trade, based on the General Agreement on Trade in Services (GATS) modes of supply. In a broad sense, these "freedom principles" include free trade in transport services; the seamless transfer of capital in setting up transport companies abroad; and the smooth movement of people, vehicles, and goods across frontiers. Freedom principles also encompass the application of most favored nation (MFN) and national treatment standards to the benefit of carriers engaged in international operations—and therefore, indirectly, to the benefit of traders.

- Harmonize and simplify technical requirements. The advantages of the most flexible market access conditions can be wiped away by applying complicated and differing technical conditions to transport operations. Onerous conditions may concern vehicle technical standards, documentation and inspection, particular and unreasonable requirements for driver competences and licenses, or the obligation to provide special certificates (in relation to the cargo or other aspects of operations). Governments are thus advised to refrain from imposing new barriers to trade in the form of technical, inspection-related, and other documentary requirements for international haulage. They should draw on existing international best practices covering the technical requirements for the vehicle, the driver, and the cargo, and simplify technical documentation requirements.

- Set harmonized and transparent rules for cross-cutting issues. International transport operations are greatly affected by general policies pursued by governments in areas like visa issuance; security rules; or insurance regulation concerning the driver, the transport operator, the vehicle, the cargo, and specific transport operations. Therefore, countries should follow international standards and set transparent rules for all these elements of the transport process. In doing so, they should take into account benefits and tools provided by existing international legal instruments and best practices to which they are or should become contracting parties (CPs).

- Nurture effective institutional and implementation arrangements. The implementation of bilateral (and multilateral) agreements depends to a large extent on efficient institutional support. This is particularly important to the decision-making processes of forging international instruments, including the effectiveness of Joint Committees (JCs) (for bilateral) or of Working Parties (for multilateral). Attention should be paid to institution building and training of officials engaged in the negotiation and administration of bilateral agreements on road transport. Better training and institutions will enable them to draft and properly implement efficient international agreements and apply the best practices existing on the international scene in this respect.

- Conform with major international obligations. Most countries are CPs to a multitude of international agreements, whether bilateral or multilateral. They should therefore consider thoroughly the rights and obligations stemming from all their international treaties when preparing, negotiating and implementing new bilateral road transport agreements. Furthermore, countries should take into account provisions of all relevant bilateral agreements they have concluded between themselves on issues that may be interrelated. Awareness of existing international obligations will allow countries to optimize their work and comply with the overall legal context. Further, any international document to which a country becomes contracting party represents a commitment and must be observed. "A party may not invoke the provisions of its internal law as justification for its failure to perform a treaty" (Vienna Convention on the Law of Treaties, article 27).

Conclusion

Lack of consistency and transparency in bilateral agreements reduces efficiency and increases cost of international road transport services. Road transport services are an extremely important part of international commerce. However, they are currently regulated by a complex mix of national, bilateral, and multilateral instruments. This promotes inefficiency and increases costs of compliance by cross-border trucking service providers. It is important to be able to assess individual agreements and identify where they may depart from international best practice or from provisions that encourage greater efficiency in the provision and integration of services.

A robust methodology is critical to assess the provisions of bilateral agreements. In the interest of helping policy-makers navigate both the existing climate and establish best practices, the present study puts forth a systematic methodology for analyzing bilateral agreements. The methodology enables policy makers to determine what elements relevant to international operations are addressed in an agreement and where gaps in the regulatory framework may remain. Such analysis can form the foundation for assessing the likely implications or included or excluded elements in any agreement.

Even more importantly, a comprehensive approach to reform the regulation of international road transport services is needed. A major weakness in attempts to help (re)establish the equilibrium between transport operators of two countries—or with attempts to reform and transform international road transport services—has been the lack of a tool to help guide analysis of existing instruments. Based on the findings of the study it is apparent that there is need for a guide to reform to sharpen the focus on efficiency in the regulation of international road transport services. The guide, in the form of a model can help focus on core elements that impact the management of international relations in road transport, particularly for freight. A well-considered and flexible model is required so it can be used to draft agreements between countries that may have different levels of development and economic integration. The development of such a model is important, but was beyond the scope of the current study. Future work in this area will therefore be directed at identifying options and paths to greater road freight transport integration especially in developing regions.

Note

1. http://untreaty.un.org/ilc/texts/instruments/english/conventions/1_1_1969.pdf.

CHAPTER 1

Introduction

Road freight transport is critical to domestic and international trade. It is the dominant mode of transport for overland movement of trade traffic, carrying more than 80 percent of traffic in most regions. Generally, nearly all trade traffic is carried by road at some point. Therefore, the cost and quality of road transport services is of critical importance to trade competitiveness of countries and regions within countries. In fact, road transport is fundamental to modern international division of labor and supply-chain management.

As infrastructure has improved across most of the developing world, regulatory and procedural constraints faced in logistics services have become more pronounced. Research in Africa and South Asia suggests that regional trade and transport corridors with limited competition in road transport services face higher prices than corridors with more competition (Chemonics International 2011; Teravaninthorn and Raballand 2009). It has therefore become important for the World Bank and other agencies to invest in regulatory reform in the logistics services sector (including trucking, warehousing, and freight forwarding) if trade costs are to be reduced. Clearly, investing only in infrastructure or trade-facilitation initiatives will not lead to significant reductions in trade costs unless they are accompanied by meaningful services reform, especially in road transport services (Borchert, Gootiiz, and Mattoo 2010; World Bank 2011).

Research on international road transport services suggests that quantity restrictions are one of the major constraints to reducing transport costs. A common recommendation from research on road transport is to establish the actual effect of the regulatory barriers between countries and the effects permit and quota systems have on the supply and costs of transport services between countries. For example, Teravaninthorn and Raballand (2009) recommended a review of bilateral agreements, among other issues, as a means of reducing transport costs in Africa. In Southern Africa freight forwarders have long argued that bilateral agreements, although seemingly sound, have inadequate management procedures that render them unsuited to the provision of efficient transport services (Nick Poree Associates 2010).

This study applies a rigorous approach to international trade-related operations and regulatory provisions that have an impact on regional and global road transport markets. While there is growing attention being paid to the political economy of road transport services, it has always been difficult to separate constraints that are founded in interstate agreements from those that are imposed through other means.

The provision of international road transport services, especially for freight, is typically regulated and supposedly facilitated by bilateral road transportation agreements. However, recent analytical work suggests that certain types of agreements have a negative effect on trade and are a major source of trade cost. Anecdotal evidence even suggests that these agreements eventually supersede more open agreements enacted at the regional level.

Although bilateral agreements have long been the traditional way of regulating the transport of passenger and freight internationally, their nature, content, and significance have not been thoroughly documented so far. Analysis of regulatory regimes for road transport has often been focused on regional or multilateral road transport facilitation agreements, which are habitually too general to be effective. Governments in the region concerned formally accede to such agreements regularly, and often this is considered to be a remarkable achievement of regional diplomatic efforts. However, the level of their practical implementation often lags behind the minimum effectiveness and efficiency requirements.

Bilateral agreements gain in importance in times of economic difficulties, as is the case of the present financial crisis in most parts of the world. In such times, governments become more inward looking and give preference to legal instruments, such as their "own" bilateral agreements. Bilateral agreements are easy for governments to "keep under control," even if they may contradict provisions of multilateral solutions adopted by the same governments at regional or even global levels (such as agreements of the World Trade Organization [WTO] or of the World Customs Organization [WCO]).

Given the continuing importance of bilateral agreements, this study was conducted with the following goals to:

- Establish and utilize a database of bilateral agreements to develop a typology of road freight transport agreements based on their restrictiveness.
- Assess the available bilateral agreements and draw conclusions, if possible, for the regional patterns in the integration of road transport markets.
- Identify any major patterns of restrictiveness of bilateral road transport agreements in different subregions and how such restrictions tend to impact road freight transport costs.
- Provide an assessment tool to guide the assessment of bilateral road transport regulatory regimes on international trade corridors.

This study was carried out through 2011 and targeted some 77 bilateral road freight transport agreements around the world with the purpose of establishing their degree of openness/restrictiveness. This information is of great importance for the smooth flow of international road freight traffic and thus the flow of international trade.

CHAPTER 2

Navigating the Bowl of Bilateral Agreements

Definition and Guidance

Bilateral agreements are treaties concluded between sovereign states and have a fundamental role in developing peaceful cooperation among nations. Treaties are regulated by the Vienna Convention on the Law of Treaties,[1] which codified the customary rules that existed in the field of treaties before 1969, the year when the Convention was concluded. The Vienna Convention on the Law of Treaties (Vienna Convention) has become a very important element of the contemporary international legal order, and has been widely recognized as the authoritative guide to the customary international law governing treaty interpretation, even by noncontracting parties to it (see map 2.1 and box 2.1).

Map 2.1 The Geographical Distribution of the 111 Contracting Parties to the Vienna Convention

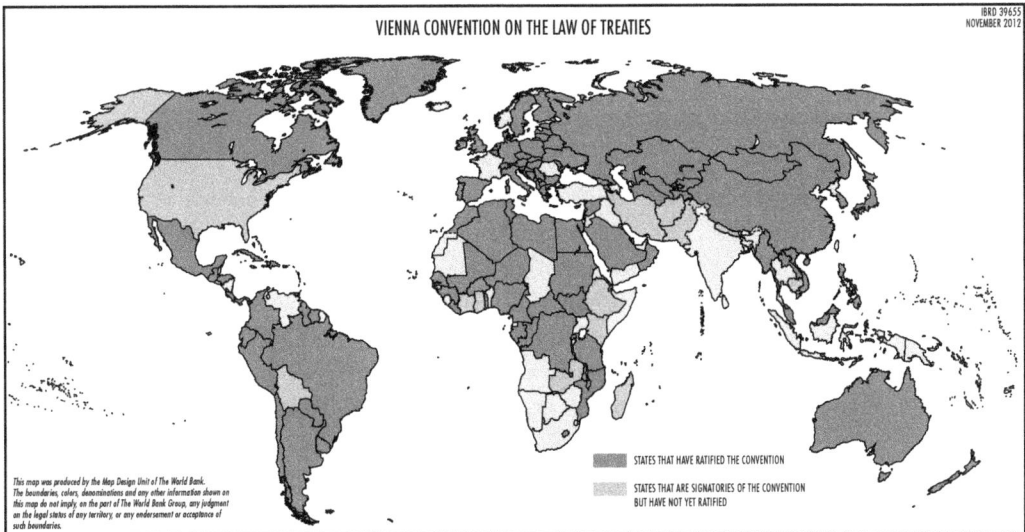

Source: World Bank.

Box 2.1

Principles of the Vienna Convention of Relevance to This Study

The Convention provides that "Every State possesses capacity to conclude treaties" (article 6) and "Every treaty in force is binding upon the parties to it and must be performed by them in good faith" ("Pacta sunt servanda") (article 26).

Other pertinent provisions include:

- On internal law and observance of treaties: "A party may not invoke the provisions of its internal law as justification for its failure to perform a treaty. This rule is without prejudice to article 46" (article 27). [Article 46 basically states that in order to invalidate its consent to be bound by a treaty a State may not invoke the fact that the consent has been expressed in violation of a provision of its internal law regarding competence to conclude treaties.]
- On the territorial scope of treaties: "Unless a different intention appears from the treaty or is otherwise established, a treaty is binding upon each party in respect of its entire territory" (article 29).
- On treaties conflicting with a peremptory norm of general international law ("jus cogens"): "A treaty is void if, at the time of its conclusion, it conflicts with a peremptory norm of general international law. For the purposes of the present Convention, a peremptory norm of general international law is a norm accepted and recognized by the international community of States as a whole as a norm from which no derogation is permitted and which can be modified only by a subsequent norm of general international law having the same character" (article 53).
- On the registration and publication of treaties: "1. Treaties shall, after their entry into force, be transmitted to the Secretariat of the United Nations for registration or filing and recording, as the case may be, and for publication; and 2. The designation of a depositary shall constitute authorization for it to perform the acts specified in the preceding paragraph" (article 80).

Source: World Bank; Vienna Convention. http://untreaty.un.org/ilc/texts/instruments/english/conventions/1_1_1969.pdf.

Bilateral agreements may regulate specific or general aspects of parties' relations: economic, financial, social, technical, and so forth. They encompass sets of rules, norms, standards, institutional arrangements, and practices accepted by the parties and are supposed to provide a comprehensive framework for the functioning of the area covered by the agreement. Under a simplified view of the hierarchy of treaties, it would appear that bilateral road transport agreements are the most specific international instruments in the field they cover.

Reasons for Concluding Bilateral Agreements

The reasons for concluding bilateral agreements on road transport are usually not openly stated in the preambles of the agreements analyzed in the study. For instance, Box 2.2 gives examples of contextual information that is typically not reflected in the preambles to the different agreements. Were the reasons to be clearly articulated, this would be useful for better categorizing the agreements and evaluating their impact on market openness and trade. However, from the experience of the authors, there are generally two types of reasons for negotiating and concluding agreements on road transport:

- *Political*:
  - The agreement is used as a starting point to develop or improve the relations between the two countries. In other words, such an agreement would represent an economic (partial) solution to a political problem.

- *Economic*:
  - To carry trade exchanges in an equitable manner (if transport capacity is unbalanced between the two parties and needs to be regulated to avoid social problems)
  - To send a signal to markets and develop demand
  - In case of large investments performed in infrastructure, to promote its use, including the development of ancillary activities
  - To detail the implementation of broader commitments assumed by the two negotiating parties in international multilateral legal instruments. For example, there are free trade agreements under which countries do not implement evenly their road transport commitments, but rather prefer to set road transport issues at the bilateral level.

All the means used for improving cooperation between countries are good. However, from an economic efficiency perspective, the main reason for concluding bilateral road transport agreements should be to promote and facilitate trade with the other country (or countries) concerned, and to satisfy the real demand from those in need of transport and transit rights—for example, traders, manufacturers, and tour and transport operators. Negotiations should only start after thorough analysis of the benefits, implications, and major interest for the national economy. Last but not least, the capacity of all parties for implementation and enforcement should be carefully and responsibly assessed in order to avoid malfunctions or nonperformance of the agreement.

The overarching goal of any negotiation carried out in good faith should be to reach "the fair compromise." The big (understandable) dilemma even of those negotiating a bilateral road transport agreement in good faith remains how to be honest while protecting national interest. It is not uncommon for one party to try to give minimum access to its national market in exchange of getting maximum access to the other party's market, in which case of course "good faith" remains empty words.

The World Trade Organization (WTO) through the General Agreement on Trade in Services (GATS) covers road transport services. However, there are few market access and national treatment commitments in this sector, as well as numerous most favored nation (MFN) exemptions to protect bilateral agreements. In other words, the basic principles of the WTO/GATS often are not

Box 2.2

Reasons for Concluding Bilateral Agreements

Malawi, Zimbabwe, and Zambia are landlocked countries in Southern Africa; each of them concluded a bilateral road transport agreement with South Africa, reflecting their strong interests in relation with this country. The agreements between them are based on the Southern African Transport and Communications Commission (SATCC) model. Besides being associated in various initiatives at regional and subregional levels, the four countries had very specific reasons for concluding bilateral road transport agreements. South Africa is Malawi's largest trade partner (the traffic between the two countries has to transit through Mozambique and Zimbabwe). Zimbabwe is heavily dependent on South African ports for its international trade. The two countries have a long history of bilateral cooperation in transport and some transport firms tend to register fleets in both countries. The countries are the only two in Southern Africa that agreed to allow cabotage, albeit on a reciprocal basis and for a limited period of time. However, cabotage is dealt with not in the bilateral agreement but rather in each country's domestic legislation. Zambia's largest trade partner is South Africa while the latter's ports are Zambia's main trade gateways (the traffic has to transit through either Botswana or Zimbabwe).

There are agreements between distant countries that are well-functioning because trade volumes keep them relevant. For example, the trade between Kazakhstan and the Netherlands amounts to US$5.2 billion, and trade between Kazakhstan and Switzerland amounts to US$11.5 billion. In the case of the agreement between the former Yugoslav Republic of Macedonia (landlocked) and the United Kingdom, 5 percent of FYR Macedonia's imports originate in the United Kingdom and are transported mainly by road.

For a long time Greece, a member of the European Union (EU), was separated from the "geographically compact" EU by countries that were not members of the Union. To facilitate Greek carriers' access to Western Europe the European Commission has negotiated transport or just transit agreements with some of the transit countries, such as the FYR Macedonia and Romania. Although it would be unfair to characterize the reasons for such agreements to only this issue, Greece's connectivity was actually the driving force of the negotiations.

Source: World Bank.

effectively applied to the road transport services sector. For the foreseeable future, bilateral agreements will remain strategic transport and trade integration tools for most countries; in fact they are among the first agreements any country concludes in establishing trade relationships with other nations. For example, in the immediate aftermath of the break-up of the former Soviet Union, almost all the newly independent states (1) became members of many international organizations or groupings, (2) acceded to international multilateral legal instruments, and (3) established dozens of bilateral road transport agreements (World Bank 2012).

Challenges and Issues

The regulation of road transport has its roots in the 1930s, when governments sought to protect the railways from competition by introducing systems of licenses, quotas, and tariffs for road transport (WTO 2010). These practices prevailed until two waves of deregulation that occurred in the 1960s and the 1980s, especially the latter. In the 1980s there was evidence that despite the controls rail transport was experiencing an ongoing erosion of traffic volumes to road transport. In the early 1980s the United States, the United Kingdom, and Europe in general introduced deregulation of transport services across the various modes (especially road and air). In Europe this eventually included definition of qualitative criteria for entry into the road transport profession and to the market, harmonization of driving and rest times, and vehicle weights and dimensions. These criteria resulted in fair competition, price deregulation, abolition of intra-Community quotas, progressive liberalization of cabotage, and other reforms. Nearly all regions of the world subsequently followed suit, at least with respect to their domestic quantitative regulatory and mandatory pricing systems for transport services.

The introduction of qualitative criteria for access to the road transport profession and market ("domestic liberalization") of transport services had a significant impact on prices. The effects of the domestic liberalization of road transport services were mainly positive and included a fall in prices, the emergence of new operators, an acceleration of concentration and specialization, a decline in the profitability of the sector, an adaptation of services to market demand, job creation, but also a relative decline in wages, bankruptcies (WTO 2010), and absorption of independent small operators by big companies. Arvis, Raballand, and Marteau (2010) point to a nexus between regulation and transport prices. They suggest that regulatory reform will decrease transport prices in a competitive market, but only if it also increases the utilization of trucks.

Quantitative restrictions are a major component of how bilateral and some multilateral agreements are implemented. Bilateral agreements typically restrict the number of vehicles allowed to provide services between the two countries. The restrictions are administered through permits designed to ensure equity of participation in the transport markets of the respective countries, and to limit the activities of other, third-country, foreign carriers. Countries prefer these agreements in part because they are easy to negotiate and manage. However, the management of quantity regulation brings with it institutions, procedures, documentation, conditions, and penalties, the cost of which is borne by the road transport industry. The most common implementing structures may involve ministries in charge of transport, foreign affairs, or communications; road regulators/agencies; road infrastructure administrations; border agencies; chambers of commerce; and associations of transport operators. The process of obtaining a permit can be burdensome, discretionary, and paper-based; it can require the physical presence of the transport operator, who may need to travel long distances from his home base to the place of distribution of permits. This process can also be straightforward; this is mostly the case in environments that are enabling business—for example, where procedures are computerized and transport operators are admitted to the profession and to the market based on qualitative criteria.

Transport companies may try to circumvent difficult permit and quota systems through cooperation between them, investment in foreign transport companies, or by setting up depots in different countries. Such companies combine GATS Modes of Supply 1 and 3 with respect to the supply of road transport services.[2]

While bilateral agreements are widely used, their design and implementation present a number of problems that have not been systematically assessed:

- **There are multitudes of bilateral agreements.** A survey carried out by the European Conference of Ministers of Transport (ECMT)[3] in 2002 found around 1,400 bilateral agreements in force, concluded between 43 European countries (WTO 2010). Sixty percent of the agreements were with third countries in Europe while the rest were with other partners. Bilateral road transport agreements account for more than 95 percent of road transport operations between EU states and third countries. For operators, keeping track of all the agreements can be a significant regulatory burden, especially given that any service between more than two countries would involve at least two agreements but likely more than two.
- **There appears to be little consistency in the content of bilateral agreements.** Except in a couple of regions identified below, there is no international pattern or set of agreed policy guidelines on bilateral agreements. It is not unusual for a country and any two parties to have agreements that are very different from each other. It is therefore quite common for traffic rights exercised over more than two countries to involve a chain of bilateral agreements, adding to the regulatory burden.
- **There is often unequal treatment of operators based on their country of registration.** Bilateral agreements are guided by principles of reciprocity and territoriality. The former refers to how CPs mirror each other's commitments and facilities and the latter to how operators have to respect the rules and conditions in force in the other contracting party.
- **Some of the bilateral agreements are quite old, and compliance with them may or may not be actively enforced.** Such agreements may lack, for example, modern provisions on protection of the environment, road safety, security, or access to the profession of road transport operator, thereby perpetuating unsustainable practices.
- **Some agreements set new technical and environmental standards that restrict market access for noncompliant transport operators.** For example, until late in the mid-2000s, Austria had bilateral road transport agreements with its Central

and Eastern European neighbors that promoted more environmentally friendly modes of transport. Such modes were promoted by sanctioning trucks travelling on their own-wheels (therefore polluting) and rewarding transport operators that used multimodal possibilities such as the ROLA ("truck-on-train"). However, the strict environmental standards in these bilateral agreements resulted in a very limited number of transit permits being issued across Austria. Traders and transport operators had to take dramatic steps to counter the highly restrictive conditions—for example, choosing deviating routes at significant higher costs.

- **Restrictive bilateral agreements can introduce market distortions and increase costs.** Where bilateral agreements are based on a quota system, the common practice is to fix the number of permits at the same level for both parties. However, if one party has bigger trade volumes or more efficient operators, then it may exhaust its quota faster than the other party.[4] Unless the quota is increased, the party with higher volume must pay for additional permits and access to infrastructure. This in turn increases the cost of transport and implicitly raises trade costs between the countries.

The various issues mentioned above manifest in operational constraints that affect the level of integration of road transport markets. Lack of bilateral agreements translates into obstacles to trade, including successive unloading and loading operations at each border crossing. On the other hand, restrictive agreements do not significantly improve the situation. Restrictions on operators of one country in foreign territories can make it impossible to load and unload cargo; fragment supply chains; and increase costs, transit times, and uncertainty in cargo flows. Operators also find it difficult to comply with varying requirements in different markets, and a company's efficient operations in one country may not create positive spillover effects in another country. Fragmented requirements may also encourage and sustain other tendencies that make integration difficult, such as low levels of standardization of equipment and operational practices.

Notes

1. http://untreaty.un.org/ilc/texts/instruments/english/conventions/1_1_1969.pdf.
2. The GATS defines trade in services by their modes of supply: (1) cross-border supply, (2) consumption abroad, (3) commercial presence, and (4) movement of natural persons.
3. The ECMT is now the International Transport Forum (ITF).
4. This was the case in the agreement between Thailand and the Lao People's Democratic Republic in the mid-2000s, when Thai operators ended up dominating the bilateral trade traffic. This has been for many years (and continues to be) the case between Romania and Turkey, where imbalance in the number of permits exchanged by the parties penalizes the road transport industry.

CHAPTER 3

Methodology

A robust analytical approach is critical to the assessment and comparison of legal texts. At best such an approach should be quantitative. The quantitative analysis of legal texts has been used in a variety of contexts, including the Quantitative Air Services Agreement Review (QUASAR) initiative of the World Trade Organization (WTO 2006) on bilateral air transport service agreements, and Law and Versteeg's work on a comparison of the constitutions of countries (Law and Versteeg 2012). In particular, this study draws on the QUASAR assessment. The WTO's QUASAR approach focused on scheduled air passenger services and sought to offer a detailed and, as far as possible, comprehensive analysis of market access features of bilateral air services agreements (ASAs). QUASAR combined both a methodology and a database of information drawn from a variety of sources. Much the same approach was utilized for the current study.

Obviously there are differences between air transport and road transport that the proposed assessment has to take into account. For instance, in road transport, factors outside the bilateral agreements have a significant impact on the conditions of traffic.[1] As such, the four-step process described below adapts the QUASAR approach to incorporate the peculiarities of road transport and especially technical requirements in road operations. The intention is to capture the various conditions that affect cross-border services along any given route.

A four-step process was utilized for the review of bilateral agreements on road freight transport:

1. Develop an analytical template and use it to eventually generate an index of openness of cross-border road transport markets.
2. Select benchmarks to compare the relative openness of each agreement.
3. Select agreements to review.
4. Conduct a statistical analysis that combines the results of the three previous steps with data on traffic between selected pairs of countries. The statistical analysis seeks to assess the relationship between demand for road transport services (as reflected in trade volumes) and the openness of the bilateral agreements between pairs of countries.

Exploring the Openness of Bilateral Agreements

In order to establish the use of bilateral agreements as a possibly valid indicator for market openness, the first step is to assess openness of individual agreements. Fundamental to this stage was the construction of a template to be used to review the agreements. The effort to establish a comparable set of agreement features made it imperative to identify the most outstanding openness aspects for the ranking/quantification exercise. The 11 features deemed important were the following:

1. Limitations of the scope of the agreement
2. Transport authorization requirements and complexities/restrictions of transport permit management
3. List of types of traffic exempted from permit requirements
4. List of types of traffic exempted from quota requirements
5. Cabotage traffic limitations
6. Transit quota limitations
7. Third-country traffic limitations
8. Prescribed routes and border crossing points
9. Taxation-related limitations
10. Facilitation measures (driver, vehicle, cargo) in place
11. Transparency requirements.

The template for the analysis was designed and tested on a small sample of agreements. Based on the results a "typology" was constructed in the form of a questionnaire (appendix A). The "Typology Questionnaire" was then used for the detailed analysis of individual agreements. Integral to the typology was the concept of a "model" agreement, deemed fundamental to the analytical approach. The "ideal" model agreement is one that does not contain restrictive provisions, at least in respect of the selected features. The level of openness of individual bilateral agreements can then be evaluated through a comparison of its features with the model agreement, which would represent the upper end of an open regime. Further, the upper-end "ideal model" would be neutral from a geographic point of view in that it would be acceptable and implementable in any region of the world. In contrast, the "lower-end" benchmark would be equal to the agreement considered to be the "worst"—that is, the least open one of the bilateral agreement databank subject to analysis.

As indicated above, the typology Questionnaire can serve as a basic template for detailed agreement investigation. The 100 questions and subquestions that were drawn cover almost all aspects of bilateral agreements and their implementation, whether of a formal or substantial nature. The results of the Questionnaire can be used to develop an instrument for "easy analysis" of further bilateral or other regional and multilateral road transport agreements.

Based on the core features identified above, the following main sections of the final Typology Questionnaire (appendix A) were defined:

1. **Basic data:** contracting parties (CPs), dates of signature and entry into force, relationship with other legal instruments, and so forth
2. **Coverage:** geographic and functional scope of the agreement, possible limitations of scope, and so forth
3. **Permit/authorization system:** traffic types subject/exempt to/from permits/quotas, types of prohibited transport, mechanism of permit delivery, quota fixing arrangements, types of permits issued, and so forth
4. **Provisions on transit:** transit permits/quotas, and so forth
5. **Triangular quotas** (third-country traffic quotas): restrictions on triangular operations, and so forth
6. **Prescribed routes:** limitation of route selection by operators to routes prescribed by authorities of the CPs, route specification, transit route facilities, and so forth
7. **Fiscal measures:** tax exemptions, tolls and duties, and so forth
8. **Vehicles and drivers:** vehicle technical requirements, vehicle certification, driving licenses, driving/rest time, driver certification, and so forth
9. **Transport operator:** insurance, liability, and so forth
10. **Specific facilitation and other matters:** nondiscrimination, protection of the environment, traffic safety, transport security, and so forth
11. **Implementation arrangements:** Joint committee (JC), infringements, and so forth
12. **Agreement final provisions:** UN registration of agreement, dispute settlement, entry into force, duration, amendment, authentic language, and so forth
13. **Scoring summary of the agreement:** list of benchmark features and their weights, boxes for attributed partial scores by features, and total score for the agreement
14. **Economic importance of agreement and proximity/adjacency factor:** traffic/trade/vehicle fleet data, economic importance of agreements, geographic data (distance in kilometers, topography, number of in-between transit countries, calculated virtual distance, and so forth.

The various features would not all have the same effect on the openness of the regulatory environment for cross-border road transport operations; it was therefore necessary to assign them weights. These weights were determined through an iterative process that involved consultations with a team of experts from various national road transport associations and one national chamber of industries,[2] as well as authors' knowledge of the industry and empirical evidence. Issues that affected each core item's weighting are discussed below.

1. **Limitations of the scope of the agreement** (maximum score: 5). The carriage of certain types of cargo may be forbidden, such as dangerous goods.

Furthermore, there might be geographic limitations of the scope of the agreement. For example, trucks of one CP may penetrate the territory of the other CP only to a certain point where trans-loading of cargo can take place. It is also possible that certain regions of the territory of one CP are excluded from the scope of the agreement. Note that all agreements, whether bilateral or multilateral, are obviously restricted in their geographic scope to the territory of the CPs only; which in this paper has not been considered geographic limitation of scope.

2. **Transport permit/authorization requirements and complexities/restrictions of transport permit management** (maximum score: 15). Any permit requirement may without doubt lead to quantitative restrictions of the number of trips feasible within a given period of time. Furthermore, determination of the number of bilaterally exchanged permits and the techniques of permit delivery/bureaucracy can make life difficult for transport operators. Various conditions of permit use may also be burdensome and of a restrictive nature.

3. **List of types of traffic exempted from permit requirements** (maximum score: 10). The list of bilaterally agreed, permit-free transport operations, if it exists, clearly indicates whether the CPs intend to facilitate operations of a noncommercial nature. The value of a list of permit-free operations is particularly high if otherwise a general permit/quota obligation applies under the scope of the bilateral agreement.

4. **List of types of traffic exempted from quota requirements** (maximum score: 8). In cases where a permit system is applicable together with restrictive quotas, it important to list any type of traffic, normally of noncommercial nature but subject to the permit system, that is at least exempt from quota limitations.

5. **Cabotage traffic limitations** (maximum score: 5). Cabotage transport (transport between two internal points in the territory of one CP by operators registered in the territory of the other CP), if allowed, may well help reduce empty runs of vehicles between two international operations. This is of some relevance for the analysis.

6. **Transit quota limitations** (maximum score: 15). Particular attention should be paid to any quantitative restrictions of transit traffic. An open-ended transit traffic regime should be appreciated by attributing a high mark. This issue should be analyzed in the light of Article 5 of the GATT[3] on the freedom of transit, which does not tolerate any quantitative restrictions of this type of traffic.

7. **Triangular/third-country traffic limitations** (maximum score: 9). Mutual enactment of triangular freight transport operations is an effective way to increase the efficiency of operations. It helps increase the share of laden runs, thus facilitating trade transactions through reduced transport costs.

8. **Prescribed routes and border crossing points** (maximum score: 8). Operators can optimize their freight runs when given the freedom to choose the most convenient route on the basis of traffic, transport technology, and trade

requirements, and factoring in possible physical infrastructure limitations. Restrictions on route choice may diminish the flexibility and quality of operations, and would run against provisions of GATT Article 5.

9. **Taxation-related limitations** (maximum score: 8). If CPs impose taxes, charges, and fees on international road freight transport operations, then these should be reasonable and proportionate duly considering relevant provisions of Article 5 of the GATT. Ideally, mutual tax and duty exemptions apply on the transport operation, the vehicles, and so forth used for such activities. Transit taxes as such cannot be tolerated.

10. **Facilitation measures (driver, vehicle, cargo) in place** (maximum score: 10). Practical facilitation measures include the acceptance of international weight and vehicle technical inspection certificates, the rapid issuance of visas to professional drivers, smooth border crossing operations, and the strict application of the nondiscrimination principle. They are all of high relevance for efficient and reliable international road freight transport operations.

11. **Transparency requirements in place** (maximum score: 7). Exchange of information on changes in national legislation, border crossing requirements, and many other circumstances of international road freight transport is indispensible in today's rapidly evolving commercial environment. Ideally, decisions of the JC in charge of the implementation of the agreement should be accessible to all actors. Methods of dispute settlement between CPs, including the possibility of appeal against measures in case of infringements, should be parts of a bilateral agreement.

In order to evaluate agreements and establish their ranking with a maximum of objectivity, it was necessary to assign "in-between values" to restrictive elements of agreements. These in-between values were used as "penalty points" against the weights of core items. These restrictive elements and their quantitative expression in penalty points are described below.

The Ideal Model and In-between Feature Values

The "ideal model" proposed here is composed of the 11 core features together with the main in-between values along an appreciation scale of 0–100. In-between values would be used as subtractive "penalty points" attributed to each undesirable feature quality (table 3.1). Thus, partial scores can be attributed to each feature, with values approaching 0 (or even negative values) for the most restrictive agreements and rising to 100 for the most open agreements. The sum of partial scores provides the total openness score for each agreement.

Not all questions of the Typology Questionnaire could be answered, and nor could scoring of the 11 core features be decided upon in a crystal clear manner. The main impediments to clear scoring were the blurred drafting of certain legal provisions in some agreements, the lack of certain elements of information, contradictions of reviewed texts, lack of information on decisions of JCs taken

Table 3.1 Features of the Ideal Model and Penalty Points for Restrictions

Core item	Feature	Ideal model	In-between values
1.	Limitations of scope	Maximum points: 5 • all territories of the parties fall under the scope of the agreement • no distance (or time) limitation to penetrate any of the territories of the CPs • no exclusivity of means of transport registered for one CP • no exclusivity of carriers for CPs • no totally prohibited operations • no permit time limitations of less than one year • no special authorization apart from overweight and overdimension (abnormal) cargos	• some territories excluded: (–) 2 • penetration distance (or time) limitations apply: (–) 2 • exclusivity allowed: (–) 2 • one or more operations totally prohibited: (–) 1 • permit validity less than six months: (–) 1 • special authorizations required: (–) 2
2.	Transport permit requirements, permit management	Maximum points: 15 • Bilateral traffic not subject to quota (open-ended) • permits exchanged before year-end for next year • permits not tradable • additional quotas available for modern vehicles and/or combined transport • no freight queuing (tour de rôle) for freight sharing • no double approval in individual permit procedures	• bilateral traffic subject to quotas: (–) 4 • no permit approval before beginning of the year: (–) 1 • permits tradable: (–) 3 • no additional quotas for modern vehicles and/or combined transport (–) 2 • freight queuing in place: (–) 3 • double approval of individual permits: (–) 4
3.	Traffic exempted from permits	Maximum points: 10 • a list of types of traffic exempt from permit obligation • all types of traffic listed in the questionnaire exempt from permit obligation	• no traffic exempt from permits: (–) 6 • less than 50 percent of types of traffic exempt from permits: (–) 4
4.	Traffic exempted from quotas	Maximum points: 8 • a list of types of traffic exempt from quota obligation • all types of traffic listed in the Questionnaire exempt from quota limits	• no traffic exempt from quotas: (–) 5 • less than 50 percent of types of traffic exempt from quotas: (–) 3
5.	Cabotage traffic limitations	Maximum points: 5 • cabotage allowed without any restriction (open-ended)	• cabotage prohibited: (–) 2 • cabotage restricted: (–) 1
6.	Transit quota limitations	Maximum points: 15 • transit operations allowed in an open-ended manner	• transit forbidden: (–) 10 • transit allowed with (quota) limitations: (–) 7 • no additional quotas for modern vehicles and/or combined transport (–) 2
7.	Triangular/third-country traffic limitations	Maximum points: 9 • triangular traffic allowed in an open-ended manner	• triangular traffic forbidden: (–) 7 • triangular traffic allowed with (quota) limitations: (–) 4

(table continues on next page)

Table 3.1 Features of the Ideal Model and Penalty Points for Restrictions *(continued)*

Core item	*Feature*	*Ideal model*	*In-between values*
			• triangular traffic allowed subject to route restrictions: (–) 3
			• no additional quotas for modern vehicles and/or combined transport (–) 1
8.	Prescribed routes and border crossing points	Maximum points: 8 • no prescribed routes for any operation • clear support to the development of road side services	• prescribed routes for transit and/or bilateral traffic: (–) 6 • other than infrastructure related motivations behind routes being prescribed: (–) 2 • no support to road side service development: (–) 2
9.	Taxation-related limitations	Maximum points: 8 • tax exemption in place for ownership taxes, registration taxes, taxes for running of the vehicle, and special taxes on transport services • fuel contained in built-in tankers, lubricants, and spare parts exempted of all import duty • initial and terminal legs of combined transport exempt from tolls and duties	• no tax exemptions: (–) 6 • only partial tax exemptions: (–) 2 • fuel and/or spare parts not exempt from duties: (–) 2 • initial and terminal legs of combined transport not exempt from tolls and duties: (–) 2
10.	Facilitation measures	Maximum points: 10 • reference included to vehicle weight certificate (per UN convention) • reference included to vehicle technical inspection certificate (per UN convention) • use of vehicle combination with units registered in different countries with one permit allowed • provisions related to the mutual recognition of driving licenses • carrier has the right to establish offices and/or appoint representatives and/or agencies in the territory of the other CP • nondiscriminatory treatment (of goods, vehicle, driver) clearly stated as an obligation • provisions in place on preferential facilitation measures for the driver (simplified immigration formalities such as passport/visa, driving licenses, and so forth), vehicles (registration, road worthiness, weights and dimensions, insurance), and goods (customs, quality-phytosanitary-veterinary checks); special expeditious treatment in case of transports of special cargoes (dangerous goods, livestock and perishable goods, temporary admission of certain goods and means of transport)	• no reference to vehicle weight certificate (per UN convention): (–) 1 • no reference to vehicle technical inspection certificate (per UN convention): (–) 1 • use of vehicle combination with units registered in different countries; one permit not allowed: (–) 3 • no provisions related to the mutual recognition of driving licenses: (–) 2 • agreement does not give carrier the right to establish offices and/or appoint representatives and/or agencies in the territory of the other CP: (–) 3 • nondiscriminatory treatment (of goods, vehicle, driver) not stated as an obligation: (–) 5 • not a single provision on preferential facilitation measures (–) 3

(table continues on next page)

Table 3.1   Features of the Ideal Model and Penalty Points for Restrictions *(continued)*

Core item	Feature	Ideal model	In-between values
11.	Transparency	Maximum points: 7 • JC in place • JC decisions made public • clear infringement procedure in place • right of appeal mentioned • exchange of information an obligation • registration of the agreement with the UN Secretary General prescribed • accessibility of pieces of national legislation required • dispute settlement arrangement in place • procedures of amendment in place	• no JC in place: (–) 2 • JC decisions not made public: (–) 3 • infringement procedure not in place: (–) 2 • right of appeal not mentioned: (–) 2 • exchange of information not an obligation: (–) 2 • registration of the agreement with the UN Secretary General not prescribed: (–) 1 • accessibility of pieces of national legislation not required: (–) 1 • dispute settlement arrangement not in place: (–) 1 • procedures of amendment not in place: (–) 1

Source: World Bank data.

subsequently to the conclusion of the agreement concerned, and so forth. In such cases, scoring took into account the "general atmosphere" and legal context of the agreement in question. Whenever faced with an absolutely uncertain choice between "more or less open solutions," a cautious approach was implemented, meaning that the less-open option was considered for scoring purposes.

At a later stage, it may be feasible to develop an "ideal" model agreement that can be recommended for use by different countries. The skeleton of such an ideal model has practically been defined in table 3.1. If so decided by transport policy makers, it would be possible to apply various elements of the ideal model in a phased-out or subtractive manner. This would help avoid disruptive effects on the road freight market of pairs of countries or a region.

A subtractive approach was adopted for the analysis. An "additive approach" rather than the subtractive one could just as easily be employed for this part of the analysis. However, despite a feeling of "positiveness" from the additive approach, it would not change the ranking order of the agreements. Furthermore, the requirements of the upper-end ideal model are considered to be better known and a more solid starting point for a subtractive analysis than the bottom-up additive approach starting from zero. This method has been used, for example, in QUASAR by the WTO and in the global competitiveness index by the World Economic Forum (WEF).

Admittedly, it is not difficult to apply other forms of notation of scores in order to follow the practice in other studies. For example, the World Bank, the Organisation for Economic Co-operation and Development (OECD), and the Australian Productivity Commission denote the most open regulatory regimes (less restrictive) as closest to zero, while the most restrictive are closest to 100.

Selection of Agreements for Review

The basis of the empirical analysis of bilateral road transport agreements is an extensive dataset of such agreements from across the world, compiled by the World Bank and the World Trade Organization. The dataset includes more than 140 such agreements, although there are obviously many more agreements worldwide than this. The selection of agreements was hampered by difficulties in obtaining certified copies of all bilateral agreements, the lack of reliable information about their actual legal status, and lack of data about the extent of their practical implementation. As a result, the study gives only parts of the overall picture. As such, this analysis must be seen as an "indicative study," which aims to explain the impact of one or another legal provision on the level of market and territory openness. In other words, the study tries to explain the extent to which road transport operations and implicitly trade are performed seamlessly between the countries concerned.

A representative sample of the agreements was then used to explore in detail different aspects of their openness. In total, 77 agreements were selected for analysis and the ranking/benchmarking exercise from the agreement database. As part of the project, it was planned that this database should, if possible, be extended to achieve a balanced geographic distribution of agreements (table 3.2).

However, the distribution of the available agreements by regions was not balanced. "Europe and Central Asia" was overrepresented (almost three-quarters of the available agreements), followed by "Africa" with 10 percent, including agreements signed between North African and European states; "Middle East" with roughly 10 percent; and "South Asia," "East Asia," and "South America" with 5 percent of the total. Therefore, the "geographic relations" pattern was used for grouping agreements (see tables 3.2 and 3.3) as it reflects better bilateral agreement reality, including the fact that many agreements are between countries on different continents and in different regions. That is to say, these legal instruments have interregional geo-coverage. In addition, this presentation reflects a truly more balanced geographic distribution of agreements. (See table 3.4 for

Table 3.2 Distribution of Bilateral Agreements in the Present Agreement Bank by Geographic Relation

Geographic relation[a]	Number of available agreements	% of total
Europe-Europe	70	50
Asia[b]-Europe	41	29
Africa-Europe	13	9
Asia-Asia	9	6
Africa-Africa	7	5
South America	1	1
Total	141	100

Source: World Bank data.
a. Agreement signed between countries located on continents mentioned.
b. Including Caucasian countries.

Table 3.3 Number of Bilateral Agreements Analyzed by Geographic Relation

Geographic relation	Number of selected agreements	% of total
Europe-Europe	18	23
Asia-Europe	29	38
Africa-Europe	13	17
Asia-Asia	9	12
Africa-Africa	7	9
South America	1	1
Total	77	100

Source: World Bank data.

Table 3.4 Number of Bilateral Agreements Analyzed by Geographic Region

Geographic region[a]	Number of selected agreements	% of total
Europe and Central Asia	45	59
South Asia	1	1
East Asia	0	0
Middle East	10	13
Africa	20	26
South America	1	1
Total	77	100

Source: World Bank data.

a. Intercontinental agreements have been included in less represented regions although they are not integral attributes of such regions. Therefore, numbers may be distorted.

the undesirable imbalances that occur if the "regional pattern" is applied for selected agreements.)

Whichever presentation scheme is used, some of the regions would be underrepresented, including Asia (except for Central Asia), Africa (except for South Africa), and South America. This would still be true even if all available agreements for these areas were selected for review (as they indeed have been). Efforts by the World Bank to obtain the text of more bilateral agreements for various regions of Africa and South America have produced only a few additional documents (those signed between two pairs of Central African countries).

For future purposes, it is recommended to obtain additional agreements and add them to the agreement databank. China, for example, has signed almost a dozen bilateral agreements with its neighboring countries and is party to a few regional schemes (IRU 2009). African and South American countries have also signed a number of relevant agreements.[4]

In order to mitigate the geographic imbalance of the selection as compared to the available agreements database, first preference was given to non-European relations and land-locked countries; other relations were added to complete the required sample. Many agreements in Europe had to be discarded because of the loss of relevance subsequent to EU enlargement or special legal arrangements between the EU and non-EU states. Because of constraints of the original agreement database, and despite efforts to reduce overrepresented relations, countries like Switzerland or Kazakhstan are overly represented. However, it was decided to keep them in the analysis because both are land-locked.

Although some of the agreements selected might seem "exotic," they have a good reason to be included in the selection. For example, the trade between Kazakhstan and the Netherlands amounts to US$5.2 billion and that between Kazakhstan and Switzerland to US$11.5 billion. In the case of the agreement between FYR Macedonia (also landlocked) and the United Kingdom, 5 percent of FYR Macedonia's imports originate in the United Kingdom and are transported mainly by road.

The selected 77 agreements cover 58 countries. The three most represented countries are: Kazakhstan (18 agreements/2 geo-relations); Switzerland (13/3); the Islamic Republic of Iran (6/1); Spain (6/3); Tunisia (6/1); the United Kingdom (6/3); Finland (5/3); France (5/3); and Morocco (5/1).

The list of selected specific agreements analyzed and ranked is in appendix B.

Multilateral and Model Agreements

In general, multilateral international legal instruments are elaborated under the auspices of global organizations or their specialized agencies—for example, the United Nations, World Customs Organization, International Maritime Organization, and so forth. These instruments are global or have a global vocation. Therefore, in general they contain framework provisions that are acceptable to all the members of the organization, irrespective of their level of development or geographic location. It is up to countries themselves to define more detailed implementing provisions, and this is commonly done in regional, subregional, or bilateral treaties and in national legislation. Regional and subregional treaties are frequent where countries are integrated in formal entities, but regional integration does not exclude bilateral cooperation between members.

In brief, being a CP to global treaties does not affect the possibility of a country being party to regional and subregional instruments or concluding bilateral agreements and implementing all these at national level. There is no impediment provided that national legislation does not contradict any international obligations or commitments of the country.

Bilateral road transport agreements often are not stand-alone legal documents but should be regarded in a wider international legal context. They can be tools for implementing multilateral treaties or even bilateral agreements of a more general nature—for example, when two countries sign first a broad economic agreement setting the principles and areas of cooperation.

Some regional entities have laudably endeavored to recommend model agreements to their constituency. While such agreements might simplify the negotiation process (especially in integrated groupings of countries), they might replicate weaknesses and limitations in subsequent bilateral agreements.

Table 3.5 Multilateral Transport Agreements and Other Legal Instruments by Areas as Selected for Benchmarking

Geographic region	Agreement and model title	Number of countries
Europe (including Caucasus)	Recommended Model Bilateral Agreement on Road Transport between European Conference of Ministers of Transport (ECMT) member countries	45[a]
	South-East European Cooperation Initiative (SECI) Memorandum of Understanding on the Facilitation of International Road Transport of Goods	10
Black Sea Region	Memorandum of Understanding on Facilitation of Road Transport of Goods in the BSEC Region; Black Sea Economic Cooperation (BSEC); Agreement on Multilateral Transit Permits	7
Asia (South-East Asia)	Agreement between and among the Governments of the Lao PDR, the Kingdom of Thailand, and the Socialist Republic of Vietnam for Facilitation of Cross-Border Transport of Goods and People (CBTA—Cross-Border Transport Agreement)	3
Africa	Memorandum of Understanding on Road Transportation in the Common Customs Area pursuant to the Customs Union Agreement between the Governments of Botswana, Lesotho, South Africa, and Swaziland	4
	SATCC Model Bilateral Agreement on the Regulation of Cross-Border Freight Road Transport	15
	Tripartite Agreement on Road Transport Uganda—Kenya—Tanzania	3
South America	ALADI Agreement on International Land Transport	7

Source: World Bank data.
a. The number represents the potential countries that might have used the model. There is no reliable evidence that the model proposed by the ECMT was followed by all the countries members of the organization.

Several multilateral agreements and models were considered of relevance to this review, some of which cover relatively wide geographic areas (table 3.5). Some of the multilateral and model agreements were selected and scrutinized to understand better the legal context of any bilateral "derived documents" based on them.

Notes

1. In aviation, transit can be free and open ended. This is known as aviation's "fifth freedom" and facilitation is not a real problem except over the Russian Federation, where the "fifth freedom" of the air is very marginal.

2. National experts who provided feedback on the test weights of agreement features were from the Czech Republic, the Islamic Republic of Iran, Kazakhstan, Poland, and Romania.

3. Wherever GATT is referred to, reference is also made to the Consolidated Resolution of the UNECE on the facilitation of road transport (R.E. 4), 30 April 2004 (TRANS/SC.1/2002/4/Rev.4), which has taken over all major principles of Article 5 of GATT.

4. ***Namibia-South Africa***: Agreement on the Carriage of Goods by Road; signed 16 May 1994; entered into force 16 May 1994 www.dfa.gov.za/foreign/bilateral0415.rtf

   Botswana-Zimbabwe: bilateral road transport agreement; signed 7 August 2001; http://www.panapress.com/Botswana,-Zimbabwe-sign-road-transport-agreement--13-498786-17-lang2-index.html

   East African Community: http://www.eac.int/infrastructure/index.php?option= com_docman&task=doc_details&gid=13&Itemid=70.

   West Africa: http://www.unctad.org/en/docs/ldc20032_en.pdf

   Andean Community: Decision No. 399 of 17 January 1997 codifies previous decisions that liberalize bilateral road transport between Andean Community members (Bolivia, Colombia, Ecuador, and Peru); World Trade Organisation, S/C/W/324, October 2010; http://www.oecd.org/dataoecd/60/61/46348780.pdf

CHAPTER 4

Typology of Bilateral Agreements

This chapter summarizes and analyzes the results of the survey based on the Typology Questionnaire. The agreements selected for the study were different in form and content; hence their features were grouped under generic subtitles to facilitate their comparison and scoring/ranking. The provisions were presented in groups with a general character, such as the preambular and final dispositions under "Political Provisions" and the provisions with a specific character under "Technical Provisions." Finally, the dispositions of a mixed nature, linked mainly to the enforcement of the agreement, were grouped under "Implementation Agreements."

As a consequence of grouping the elements in this comparable structure, the analysis does not follow strictly the sequence of questions appearing in the Typology Questionnaire.

Political Provisions

Political provisions in a bilateral road transport agreement are important because they can reveal the reason for concluding the agreement, the commitment to properly implement it, the commitment to further improve the situation existing at the moment of concluding the agreement, and so forth. Attention to detail should characterize such negotiations, in order to avoid disputes on interpretation and to provide the enforcers and beneficiaries (public implementing agencies, transport operators, traders) with a well-functioning tool.

The survey aimed at collecting information on the existence in the agreement of certain elements deemed important in the treaties' practice:

- **Specific aspects.** These include the identification of the contracting parties (CPs), the existence of a "definitions" chapter, the language(s) of the agreement, the option for a reference language and indication of the authentic text, the dates of signature and entry into force, the duration of the agreement, and existence of a clause of automatic extension.
- **The general context and the environment in which the agreement is concluded.** These include replacement of an older agreement by a new one, if

concluding the agreement under the umbrella of a wider framework, existence of provisions related to relationship with other treaties, and prevalent law.

- **Final dispositions.** These include the obligation to register the agreement with the Secretary General of the United Nations (according to the Charter of the United Nations, Chapter XVI, Miscellaneous Provisions, Article 102), transparency and availability of pieces of national legislation and regulations, right of appeal against decisions of competent authorities, dispute settlement arrangements, procedures of amendment of the agreement including its Annexes and/ or Protocols, and obligation or recommendation to consult the other party when reviewing national regulations relating to the agreement.

Basic Data of Agreements

The identification of the precise *denomination of the two CPs* of each agreement is an easy task, as all the selected agreements contain this element.[1] The information on the *date of concluding/signing* the agreements is available for all agreements but one. The *date of entry into force* is not available for 27 agreements (or 35 percent) out of 77. This is certainly a high level of data nonavailability. Further research is necessary to reduce this level, which would help creating more visibility of the agreements' legal status.

Eight agreements (or 10.4 percent) *replace* previous ones and just five (or 6.6 percent) have been signed under the umbrella of a *wider framework* of international agreements.

A great majority (73 agreements or 94.8 percent) contains reference to the CPs' *other international obligations* stemming from various international bi- and multilateral agreements and conventions they are parties to, which can be transport-specific or general cooperation instruments. For example, in respect of multilateral transport conventions, specific references have been found to the Customs Convention on the International Transport of Goods under Cover of TIR Carnets (TIR Convention)[2] on customs transit or the European Agreement concerning the International Carriage of Dangerous Goods by Road (ADR),[3] on road traffic, the Agreement on the International Carriage of Perishable Foodstuffs and on the Special Equipment to be used for such Carriage (ATP) Convention[4], the Agreement Concerning the Work of Crews of Vehicles engaged in International Road Transport (AETR) Convention[5] on driving and rest time rules and the application of the related on-board checking equipment (tachograph), various pieces of European Union (EU) legislation, and so forth.

Almost one-fifth of the agreements (15 or 19.5 percent) do not contain any *definition chapter* and most of the agreements define only a very limited number of terms such as "carrier," "company," "competent authorities," various types of "documents," and "vehicle." Some of them include further details like the definition of types of transport operations that can be conducted under the cover of bilateral road transport agreements.

The *language* in which each agreement was concluded is indicated in 74 agreements (or 96 percent). The majority of agreements (64 out of 74 for which this information is available or 86.5 percent) have been concluded in languages of the CPs while 64.9 percent have been worded also in an "international language," the language of reference that normally prevails in case of a divergent interpretation of the text of agreement between the CPs. Indeed, a great majority (70 out of 76 for which this information is available or 92.1 percent) contains an explicit listing of authentic languages of the agreement.

Agreement Final Provisions
Notwithstanding their importance for the clear understanding of the agreement and for its practical implementation, the final provisions are often overlooked in the bilateral road transport agreements that were analyzed. The results of our review are not too encouraging (figure 4.1).

Only one (or 1.3 percent) out of the 77 agreements contains the obligation for CPs to *register* their joint document with the Secretariat of the United Nations. This obligation derives from the Charter of the United Nations, Chapter XVI, Miscellaneous Provisions; Article 102 for the UN Member States, and from the Vienna Convention on the Law of Treaties (Article 80) for the CPs thereto. Although this obligation has not been included in the agreements, many

Figure 4.1 Distribution of Agreements by Their Final Provisions

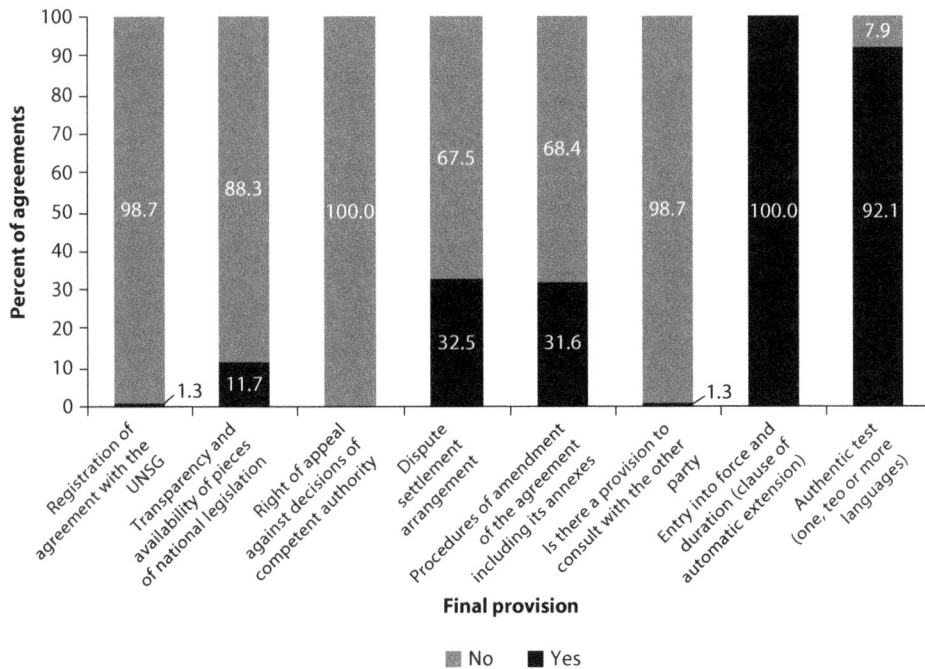

Source: World Bank data.

have been registered with the UN, following the unilateral initiative of one of the CPs. In such cases no penalty points have been applied in the ranking process.

This study would have been more comprehensive if bilateral agreements were registered as foreseen in international law, making access to the agreement databank easier. Moreover including the obligation for CPs to register their joint document with the Secretariat of the United Nations and observing it would significantly contribute to improving transparency in this field of international regulation.

Only nine agreements (or 11.7 percent) contain an explicit requirement for the accessibility of relevant *national legislation* for operators under the scope of the agreement. Similarly, only one agreement (or 1.3 percent) requires mutual consultation between the CPs before the introduction of national measures that may affect implementation.

None of the 77 agreements provides for the *right of appeal* of operators against disciplinary action by governments related to supposed infringements. This is quite a dramatic lapse. In some agreements, there is a clause stating that all the issues not settled under the agreement (including, most likely, the right of appeal) will be dealt with according to the national legislation of the parties. However, this "surrogate" clause does not offer a solution for international road transport operators. Standard national appeal deadlines often give travelling drivers or their home base little time to react, and procedures may be unknown and complex, preventing CPs from filing an appeal in due time and form.

Surprisingly, a great majority of the agreements (52 or 67.5 percent) do not regulate the *dispute settlement* between the CPs. Many potential conflicts or divergent opinions can certainly be settled by the Joint Committee (JC). However, if the JC fails to reconcile the parties or if the creation of the JC itself is not foreseen in the agreement, the ways and means of settling cooperation problems between the parties are rather opaque.

One-third only of the agreements (24 out of 76 for which this information is available or 31.6 percent) contain provisions on procedures for *amending* the agreement, which may result in uncertainties about the status of the agreement at a given moment.

Finally, all agreements reviewed settle the issue of *entry into force and duration*.

Efforts were made to exclude from the study agreements that are not in force or not implemented anymore. However, no reliable and accessible information was available during the study about whether the selected agreements are still in force and whether they have not been superseded by new agreements.

Technical Provisions

The study looked into the issues of substance that are negotiated in the frame of bilateral agreements, particularly those defining the conditions for access to the market and territory of each CP for road transport operators of the other CP. In many cases a road transport operator crossing several countries during the course of an international journey could expect to be presented with numerous forms to fill in, often asking for exactly the same information, but in a slightly different way. Additional dangers are generated by the lack of knowledge and/or proper understanding of the mutual rights and obligations of the parties involved in international transport. In such cases, small and medium-size transport companies are at higher risk as they can neither bear the legal costs incurred by infringements (including sanctions) nor afford prior legal advice to avoid such risk (see UNESCAP 2007). The technical provisions actually reflect the "fair compromise" reached after negotiations and are paramount to the success of a bilateral road transport agreement. These provisions must be detailed, clear as to avoid interpretations or abuse, transparent, and available to all interested.

The survey aimed at collecting information on the existence in the agreement of provisions that would facilitate or restrict the seamless transport and implicitly trade between the CPs, including the following:

- **Coverage:** limitations in the geographical scope of the agreement, "depth" of operations allowed (into the national territory)
- **Exclusivity:** transport services between the parties to be exclusively performed by transport operators and means of transport registered in one of the CPs
- **Restrictions:** types of transport prohibited, types of permits, quota requirements, freight allocation/queuing system, transit to/from third countries, prescribed routes, and exit/entry points for transit or any other international operation
- **Facilitation:** incentives for vehicles meeting the most modern safety and emissions standards or for the use of multimodal possibilities such as ROLA ("truck-on-train"), RORO ("truck-on-ship"), or the use of alternative routes; exemption from tolls, duties, and taxes; right to establish offices and/or appoint representatives and/or agencies in the territory of the other CP
- **Vehicles:** insurance, technical requirements, mutual recognition of weighing and technical inspection certificates of vehicles
- **Driver:** simplified immigration formalities, mutual recognition of driving licenses, special qualifications
- **Goods:** insurance, customs, quality, phytosanitary and veterinary checks, expeditious treatment for transports of special cargoes
- **Risk:** liability of the carrier, nondiscriminatory treatment (of goods, vehicle, driver), Safety: environment protection, safety and security of traffic and/or transport operation.

Coverage

None of the agreements assessed contain any limitation of the *geographic scope* of transport operations, meaning that no territories are excluded and the distance of penetration into national territories is not restricted. Just one or two agreements mention that they are not applicable for overseas territories of one of the CPs, but this information is not relevant to this study.

Only a small minority of agreements (6 out of 76 for with this information is available, or 7.9 percent) limits the *use of vehicles* or that of *transport operators* only to those registered in the territory of the two CPs (meaning exclusivity) in the context of bilateral/transit/third-country road transport operations. Such a constraint applies only in South Africa and Central Africa.

In an overwhelming majority of agreements (71 out of 76 for which this information is available, or 93.4 percent) there is at least one type of transport operation *prohibited* under the cover of the agreement. Cabotage is the type of transport that is prohibited in all but two agreements. Third-country (or triangular) operations are prohibited in 28 out of 76 agreements (or 36.8 percent) for which this information is available. There are, however, cases where both cabotage and third-country transport may take place, provided a special authorization is issued for the purpose.

In a few agreements there is an explicit list of *goods forbidden* for transport under the cover of the agreement: arms, ammunition, military equipment, and certain goods (dangerous goods, fuels, waste material) due to sanitary-phytosanitary-veterinary-security reasons. In a number of agreements, the JC is mandated to define the conditions for performing transport operations that are normally prohibited under the agreement.

The majority of agreements contain a burdensome *authorization (permit) regime* for bilateral and transit traffic (63 for bilateral and 61 for transit operation out of 75 for which this information is available, or 84 percent and 81.3 percent respectively). Around 16–19 percent allow totally permit-free (open-ended) bilateral and transit traffic.

Third-country operations, which are important from a transport efficiency point of view (reduction of empty runs), are prohibited or subject to special permits under more than half of the agreements (53.4 percent), while the other half imposes "ordinary" third-country permits.

No trace has been found of permits valid for *border region* operators in the agreements reviewed (figure 4.2).[6]

In a few cases, particular permits are required for *empty entry* into the territory of one CP territory to pick up cargo with trucks registered in the territory of the other CP. In one agreement, the pick-up of *return cargo* after unloading in the territory of one CP by trucks registered in the territory of the other CP is subject to a specific permit.

Finally, none of the agreements analyzed contains provisions that would establish a prevalence of national law over the bilateral agreement, although reportedly such cases exist. According to international law and practice of the treaties, any *national restriction on the implementation of an international agreement* should be considered as null and void.

Permit Systems

As already mentioned, there are just two agreements that allow cabotage transport without restrictions, meaning that in almost 90 percent of the agreements

Figure 4.2 Permits/Authorizations Applicable under the Agreement for Various Operations

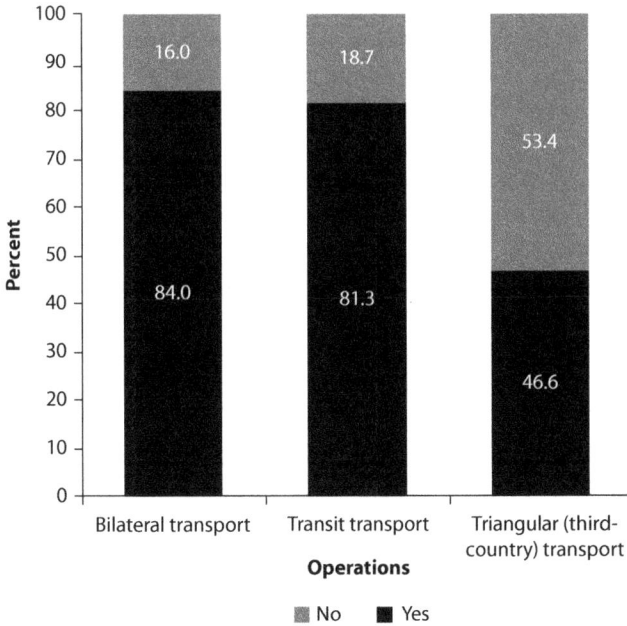

Source: World Bank data.

Figure 4.3 Cabotage Regulation in Bilateral Agreements

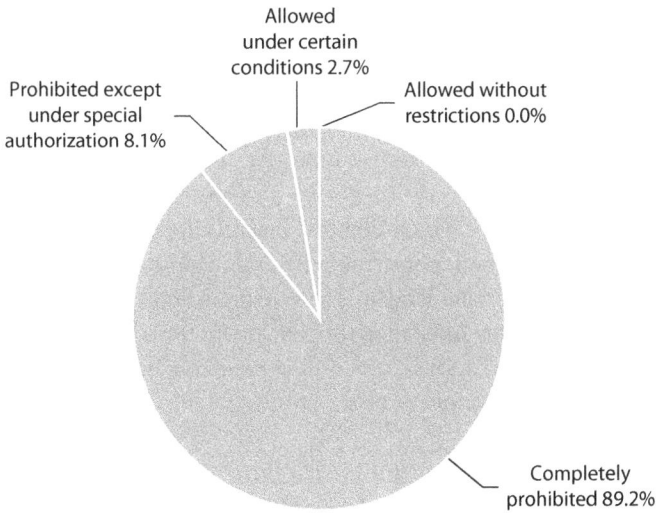

Source: World Bank data.

(66 out of 74 for which this information is available or 89.2 percent) cabotage is completely prohibited. There are only 6 agreements (or 8.1 percent) that allow cabotage, subject to a special authorization issued under conditions that are set by the JC (figure 4.3).

Compared to the rigidity of the cabotage regulation, there is much more flexibility regarding *exemptions from permit* requirements. A great majority of agreements (55 out of 70 for which this information is available or 78.6 percent) contain a list of permit-free transport of certain types of cargo even under a general obligation of using permits. Tolerant agreements in this respect are scattered over various regions. They can be found in Southern Africa, Central Asia, Europe, or in agreement relations like Africa-Europe and Asia-Europe. Road transport practice as well as international legal instruments (particularly those elaborated under the World Customs Organization)—or for certain regions multilateral agreements (like the European Conference of Ministers of Transport [ECMT] model)—may have influenced the type of exemptions applied in bilateral schemes. The most frequent exemptions are as follows:

- Transport of damaged or broken-down vehicles and transport of breakdown repair vehicles (44 agreements out of 63 agreements for which bilateral permits apply or 69.8 percent)
- Transport for noncommercial purposes of properties, accessories, and animals to or from theatrical, musical, film, sports, or circus performances (including race horses, race vehicles, and boats); fairs or fêtes; and items intended for radio recordings, or for film or television production (38 agreements out of 63 agreements for which bilateral permits apply or 60.3 percent)
- Funeral transport (38 agreements out of 63 agreements for which bilateral permits apply or 60.3 percent)
- Transport of works and objects of art for fairs and exhibitions or for noncommercial purposes (37 agreements out of 63 agreements for which bilateral permits apply or 58.7 percent)
- Transport of medical supplies and equipment needed for emergencies, particularly in response to natural disasters and humanitarian needs (34 agreements out of 63 agreements for which bilateral permits apply or 54 percent)
- Other categories like mail, household removals, transport with vehicles whose maximum permissible total weight is less than 6 tonnes or whose total payload is below 3.5 tonnes, bees and young fish, objects/material for publicity and information, animal corpses, and so forth (43 agreements out of 63 agreements for which bilateral permits apply or 68.25 percent).

Exempting certain transports from *quota* limitations is practiced in a number of agreements even if a general quota restriction applies. For example, household removal transport can often be carried out without any quota limitation (34 agreements out of 53 for which bilateral quota applies or 64.15 percent), as well as the "other categories" listed above (43 out of 53 for which bilateral quota applies or 81.1 percent). Perishable foodstuffs are exempted from quotas in a small number of agreements (7 out of 53 for which bilateral quotas apply or 13.2 percent).

Mirror (reciprocal) agreements of the permit and quota systems between CPs are almost generalized for all agreements (that is, there is symmetry). This is, however, a presumption based on general parts of texts, as the quota-sharing formula is clearly stated only in a minority of the agreements (22 out of 54 for which this information is available, or 40.7 percent). Imbalanced (asymmetric) quota sharing has clearly been identified in two agreements signed in Central Africa.

However, *no additional quota exemptions or other incentives* are applied in any of the agreements to reward the use of vehicles meeting the most modern safety and emission standards or the use of ROLA, RORO, or alternative routes. This may be partially due to the fact that the great majority of the agreements under review were signed in the 1980s (15 or 19.48 percent), the 1990s (30 or 38.96 percent) and early 2000s (18 or 23.4 percent)(figure 4.4). This was a period when rising environmental consciousness was leading to fixing and implementing permit and quota preferences linked to vehicles' environmental performance (as opposed to ROLA or RORO logistics). One well-known example is that of the former European Conference of Ministers of Transport (ECMT), which decided that the allotment of multilateral quota should give preference to transport operators using vehicles complying with high safety and emission standards.

The study finds that permit trading is not allowed for all agreements where permits are applicable. This is at least the formal legal arrangement and it can only be hoped that competent authorities are able to prevent illegal (black market) trading. No specific and confirmed information is available about anecdotal indications of illegal trading.

Figure 4.4 Distribution of Agreements by Date of Conclusion

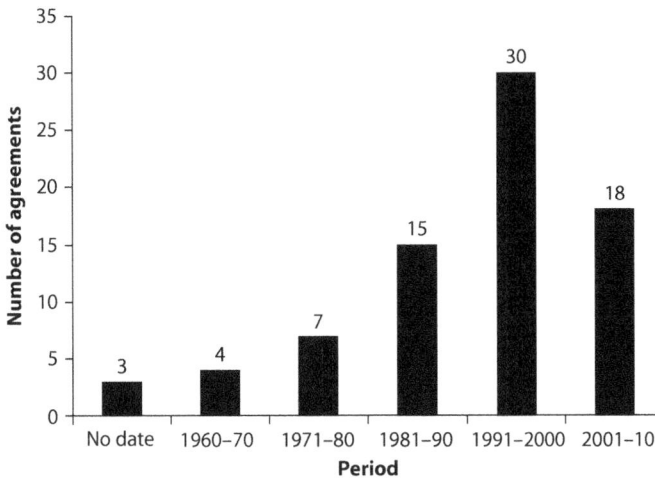

Source: World Bank data.

There are no specific requirements in any of the agreements for permit issuance, such as certification of value-added tax (VAT) status, vehicle road worthiness, operator licensing, or vehicle ownership. The use of "freight queuing" (tour de rôle), a market-sharing formula at company level, has not been traced in any of the agreements.

Provisions on Transit

An overwhelming majority of agreements (70 out of 71 for which this information is available or 98.6 percent) explicitly cover transit traffic through the territory of one CP by vehicles registered in the territory of the other CP.

Transit is forbidden in one single agreement. At the other end of the scale, it is allowed in an open-ended manner only in 22 agreements (30 percent) and is permitted with limiting transit quotas in 50 cases (69 percent). It is remarkable that the majority of the CPs wish to restrict transit transport operations, thereby restricting transport and trade relations of the other CP with third countries, thus violating General Agreement on Tariffs and Trade (GATT) Article 5 on the freedom of transit (figure 4.5).

Only one agreement allows additional transit quotas for vehicles meeting the most recent safety and emissions standards and/or for using ROLA, RORO, combined transport modes, or other alternative routes. This is similar to the lack of such incentives in respect of quotas for bilateral transport.

Triangular Quotas

As mentioned above, triangular or third-country transports can increase transport efficiency and drive down costs significantly, notably by reducing the empty backhauls. As shown above, almost half of the agreements require a

Figure 4.5 Transit Regulation in Agreements

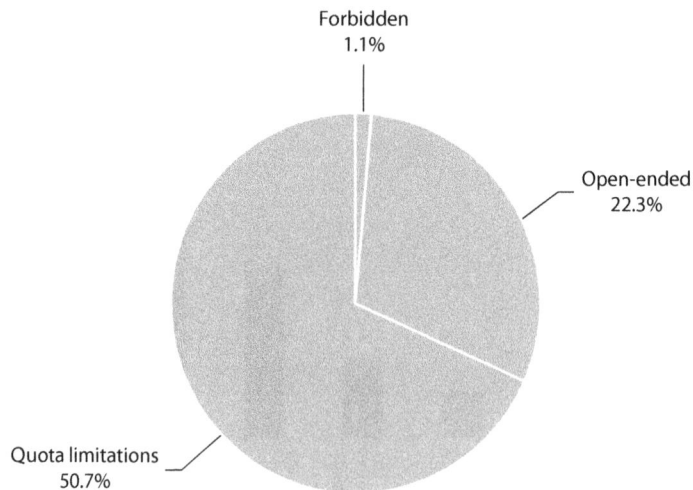

Source: World Bank data.

Figure 4.6 Triangular Quotas in Agreements

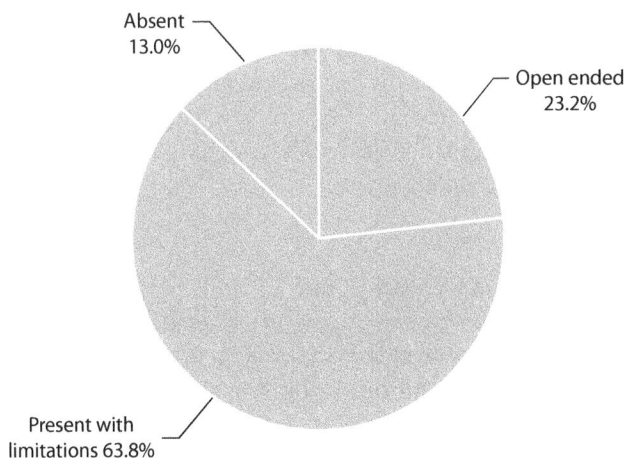

Source: World Bank data.

regular permit to carry out this type of operation; for the rest, either a permit-free regime (a minority of agreements) or special permits or simply prohibition apply. Indeed, out of 69 agreements for which this information is available, only 16 agreements do not have quantitative limitations (23.2 percent), while 44 agreements (63.8 percent) contain quota limitations. Nine agreements (13 percent) do not contain provisions related to triangular quotas (figure 4.6).

Fortunately, the so-called self-transit obligation for triangular operations (the route must pass through the territory of vehicle registration) exists only in six agreements (11.5 percent out of 52 agreements for which this information is available) allowing triangular operations. Once more, no incentives appear in any agreement but one for advanced environmental features of vehicles or involvement in combined transport operations.

Prescribed Routes

Beside triangular self-transit obligation, route restrictions have been identified in a relatively high proportion of agreements (17 or 22.1 percent), basically in South-East Asia, Central Asia, Southern and Central Africa, and South America. Only four of these specifically list the routes to be used. The agreements do not include reasons for route restrictions; moreover none of the agreements containing route restrictions stipulate mandatory technical parameters or design standards of designated roads. Similarly, none of these (or other) agreements speaks about any roadside services to be provided to road transport operators and drivers along the obligatory routes (for example, first aid, repair, fuel, telecommunications, loading/unloading, storage, restaurants and rest, parking, facilities, and so forth).

Nine agreements contain explicitly prescribed frontier crossing points. In reality, this number should be close to the number of agreements featuring route restrictions, because the designated main highways normally can be approached only through specific border crossing points. The prescription of mandatory entry/exit or border crossing points could be useful in a certain phase of development, such as during the initial period of the application of a new customs (transit) scheme. In these cases, a step-by-step lifting of border crossing constraints, simultaneously with restraints on the use of domestic highways, remains the main objective.

Fiscal Measures

Vehicles registered in the territory of one CP and circulating in the territory of the other CP are fully exempt from taxes on ownership, registration, and operation, and from special taxes on transport services, in only half of the agreements (32 out of 75 for which this information is available or 41.6 percent). They are partially exempt in 13 agreements (16.9 percent) and not exempt at all in 32 agreements (41.6 percent) (figure 4.7).

The agreements analyzed show a great variety of fiscal exemption conditions. It is frequently stated that national law applies for all fiscal matters—meaning that no joint fiscal arrangement has been reached between the CPs. In general, exemption applies most frequently for taxes on owning and running vehicles and the transport activity as such. The agreements cover various fiscal arrangements: the exemption of bilateral and transit traffic only, the exemption of bilateral and triangular but not of transit traffic, another one that lists categories of permits exempt from taxes, and a few agreements that list the names of specific taxes for which exemption applies. Many agreements state that there are no exemptions for road tolls and road user charges or the fiscal imposition (for example, VAT) on fuel consumption. One agreement allows an exemption under a certain period of stay (for example, 21 days) in the territory of the CPs. Exemptions may apply even for company revenue and profit taxes. In a number

Figure 4.7 Tax Exemption of Vehicles from the Other Party in Agreements

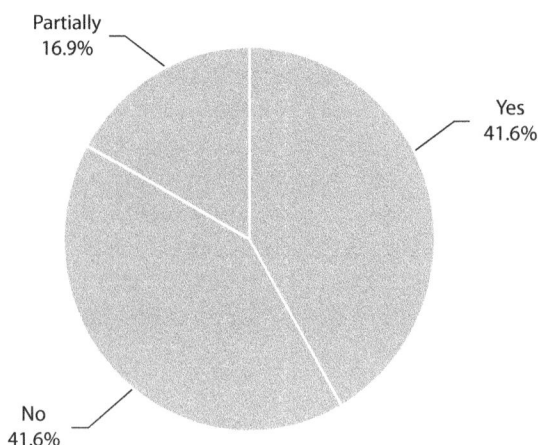

Partially
16.9%

Yes
41.6%

No
41.6%

Source: World Bank data.

of cases, fiscal conditions have been fixed in published or unpublished protocols to the agreement, or it is stated that the fiscal treatment of transports is left with the JC. Some agreements explicitly exclude any taxation on the issuance of transport permits, but no clear reference has been identified to agreements concluded between the same CPs on fiscal matters, such as the prevention of double taxation.

An important issue for operational purposes is whether fuel contained in tanks of vehicles built-in by the manufacturer, lubricants, and spare parts imported under temporary customs regime for operation and repair purposes are exempted from customs duties. This is clearly the case in 48 agreements out of 74 for which this information is available (64.9 percent), while such duty exemption does not apply for more than one-third of the agreements. None of the agreements contains any fiscal preference or incentive regarding the initial and terminal legs of combined transport operations.

Vehicles, Drivers, Transport Operators

The Typology Questionnaire contains a number of questions concerning agreement provisions on vehicles, drivers, and transport operators. A few agreements only (8 out of 76 for which this information is available or 10.5 percent) contain general *technical specifications for the vehicles* registered in the territory of one CP in order to be admitted in the territory of the other CP. However, most agreements (60 out of 75 for which this information is available or 80 percent) have additional specifications for transporting goods in vehicles whose weights and dimensions surpass the agreement's maximum permissible standards.

None of the agreements contains any reference to the multilateral UN International Convention on the Harmonization of Frontier Controls of Goods, 21 October 1982[7] ("Harmonization" Convention), particularly its Annex 8. One feature of the Harmonization Convention is the facilitation of border crossing by the mutual recognition of the international certificates on the *roadworthiness* and the *checked weight* of vehicles. However, in a few agreements in Southern Africa CPs have agreed on the bilateral recognition of national certificates issued for these two purposes. The Commonwealth of Independent States (CIS) shares a joint international weight certificate, but it is not referenced in any bilateral agreement reviewed for the CIS.

Only a minority of agreements (24 out of 70 for which this information is available or 34.3 percent) allows the use of *vehicle combinations* made up of vehicle units (tractor and trailer/semi-trailer) registered in different countries. This situation is detrimental from the point of view of flexibility of operations and the requirements for modern road transport logistics. Although there are cases when such combinations might facilitate road transport of goods, in general the authorities avoid authorizing them because they fear abuses by operators regarding the use of bilateral permits.

Driving and rest time rules for drivers have been a major item for regulation over the last 50 years, and are present in one form or another in the majority of the countries which are contracting parties to the agreements reviewed. These rules are important facilitators of road safety and fair market competition. This sensitive issue is traditionally subject to regulation by multilateral legal instruments in Europe and Central Asia. It is therefore surprising that only seven (9.2 percent) out of the 76 agreements for which this information is available make any reference to this type of multilateral regulation. However, this lack of reference does not alter the obligation of the parties to observe rules to which they may have acceded in a multilateral context.

Requirements regarding *driver qualifications* are not subject to any of the bilateral agreements.

Regarding transport *operators*, the question was raised, among others, whether or not Motor Vehicle Third-Party Insurance is obligatory. Only 19 agreements (25 percent) out of 76 for which this information is available contain such an obligation.

Operators' liability towards their clients is not subject to bilateral regulation either. It seems that CPs implicitly leave this sensitive matter to be tackled by the Convention on the Contract for the International Carriage of Goods by Road (CMR),[8] which is however mentioned by name only in a very limited number of agreements.

A few agreements (8 out of 76 for which this information is available or 10.5 percent) contain conditions for establishing company offices and/or representation bureaus/agencies in the territory of the other CP.

Specific Facilitation and Other Matters

A significant majority of agreements (44 or 57.1 percent) do not contain explicit and general provisions on the *nondiscriminatory treatment* of goods, vehicles, and drivers in the territory of the CPs. In 13 cases (16.9 percent), partial nondiscrimination clauses have been identified. This leaves only one-quarter of the agreements reviewed with the mandatory use of the nondiscrimination principle (figure 4.8).

Wherever mentioned, nondiscrimination is interpreted in respect of the application of national law, in particular on weights and dimensions of vehicles, the application of fiscal rules, road user charges, the right to take return cargo, and what is commonly referred to as the fair treatment of transport operators. Practically, nondiscrimination is understood to be the application of the national treatment (NT) principle only. The reason for this is that the mandatory use of the most favored nation (MFN) treatment would possibly be in flagrant contradiction with the bilateral character of the agreements.

Contrary to expectations, only 10 agreements (13.2 percent) out of 76 for which this information is available contain a reference to the needs of *environmental protection* and only in very general terms or in relation to vehicle pollution levels. Thirty-three agreements (43.4 percent) out of 76 contain a reference to the importance of road *safety*, mostly in the form of a call to observe traffic rules. Only one agreement contains an explicit reference to (only national)

Figure 4.8 Obligatory Nondiscriminatory Treatment of Goods, Vehicles, and Drivers in Agreements

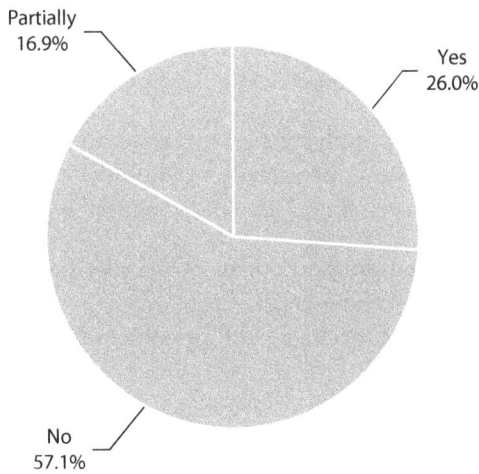

Source: World Bank data.

security considerations, while transport security as such is not included in any of the agreements.

A clear minority of agreements (22 out of 76 or 28.9 percent) deal with various specific road transport *facilitation measures,* such as unimpeded passage through frontiers, priority border checks and passage for live animals, goods for humanitarian aid, perishable and dangerous cargo; as well as accelerated visa procedures and issuance of multi-entry visa for an extended period.

A clear majority of agreements (80 percent) do not require the presence of specific documents on board other than permits that should be presented on request to checking authorities. CPs requesting additional documents ask for consignment notes, international cargo manifest, license vignette and "safe conduct" (the two latter mainly in Southern Africa), vehicle fitness and weight certificates, customs documents, spare parts list, insurance policy, vehicle carnet de passage, and so forth.

Implementation Arrangements

In general, acceding to or ratifying legal instruments or concluding a bilateral agreement are rather simple political processes, but they will not produce effects unless the instruments are properly implemented. The survey collected information on implementation provisions in agreements, including definition of roles, communication between parties, actions to be taken in case of noncompliance, and so forth. The main elements surveyed were as follows:

• **Definition of responsibilities:** competent authorities clearly nominated, competencies and functioning of the JC extensively defined

- **Practicalities of the implementation:** modalities for agreeing on the number of permits (annual quotas) and on ways of exchanging them, procedures in case of infringement
- **Exchange of information:** sharing information on issues pertaining to the implementation of the agreement.

In respect of agreements applying a permit and quota system, it is of concern that an important share (out of 65 agreement for which this information is available) does not contain any *technical details* on the following issues (figure 4.9):

- **Modalities for agreeing on the number of permits (and annual quotas):** no reference at all in 14 agreements (21.9 percent)
- **Modalities and date of exchange of permits:** no reference at all in 36 agreements (55.4 percent)
- **Conditions of permit validity:** no reference at all in 23 agreements (36.5 percent)
- **Conditions of permit use:** no reference at all in 24 agreements (36.9 percent).

Similarly, wherever *quotas* apply, they are *not specified* in the agreements (up to 87.5 percent of agreements applying bilateral quotas). In few agreements the quota limit is quantified, but this value is valid only for the first year of implementation, thereafter it is re-negotiated in the JC. The fact that in most of the cases the decisions of the Committee are not made public contributes to the opaqueness of the quota situation.

Figure 4.9 Technical Provisions Concerning Permit Management in Agreements

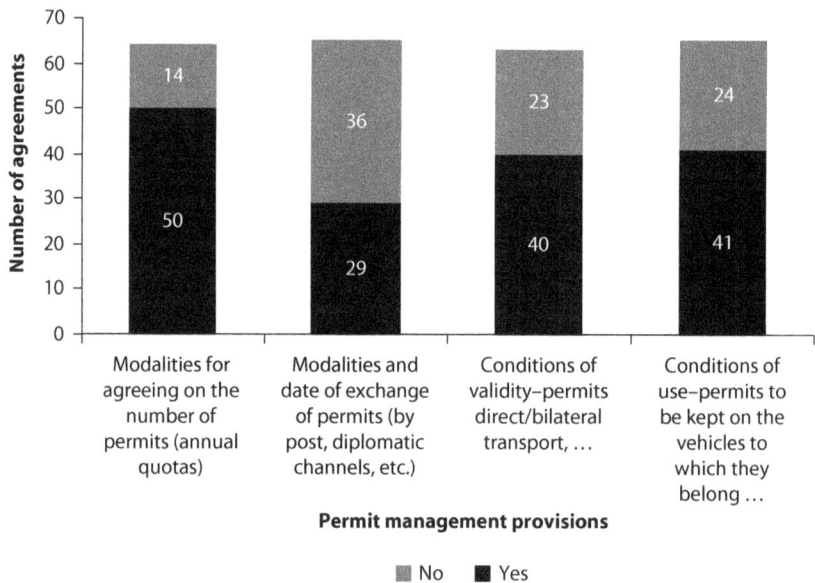

Permit management provisions

No   Yes

Source: World Bank data.

Questions have been asked about the existence of *double approval* procedure for issuing permits or fixing quotas. In the great majority of agreements double approval does not exist for permit issuing procedures (64 out of 71 for which this information is available or 90.1 percent) or quota fixing (65 out of 70 for which this information is available or 92.9 percent). For the rest of the agreements (8 or 10 percent) double approval does exist, namely in Southern Africa and South America.

Lack of information on competent authorities can certainly make life difficult for transport (and trade) operators. However one-third of the agreements (25 or 32.5 percent) do not contain any identification of competent authorities in charge of implementation (although the denomination of authorities even without any detailed contact details has already been considered as sufficient identification). This issue was likely left to either unpublished protocols of signature or equally nonpublic and legally lower-level international documents like, for example, minutes of JC meetings. A few agreements contain provisions establishing detailed responsibilities for authorities that are named as being in charge of various issues of implementation; although far from applying the "single window" principle extensively advocated over the latest decades, this is certainly a more convenient situation for practitioners.

In a great majority of cases (72 out of 76 for which this information is available or 94.2 percent) CPs have considered it important to set up a *joint committee* (JC) as a common platform to oversee agreement implementation. Decisions of most of these JCs (61 out of 65 for which this information is available or 93.8 percent) are not public. If no explicit obligation is mentioned in the agreement to publish such decisions, or if a protocol of signature or similar documents referenced in the agreement has not been attached to the agreement text, it can be understood that the contracting parties considered that such decisions should not be made public.

The decisions of JCs can be quite far-reaching, either by providing much of an agreement's wider legal framework or even by tacitly bending certain agreement provisions. Consequently, the total lack of information about their decisions was a real handicap in executing the study. However, it is unlikely that this diminishes the value of the benchmarking in quantifying the letter and spirit of international legal instruments. Nor does it reduce the study's value in checking the degree of openness of either existing or planned bilateral road transport agreements and regulations.

With only four exceptions (out of 76 for which this information is available), agreements contain *infringement provisions* against violators of the agreement or of national legislation in countries of the CPs. The most commonly used infringement procedures include such disciplinary measures as simple warnings, warnings of exclusion/suspension, and actual exclusion of drivers and/or transport operators from transports falling in the scope of the agreement. These measures are normally taken against the operator by the competent authorities in whose country the operator is registered upon request by the competent authorities in whose country the infringement has been committed. In a few agreements, however, a "reverse procedure" is defined whereby the competent authorities of the country where the violation has taken place sanction the transgressor in a direct manner according to national legislation and subsequently inform the competent authorities of the operator's country of registration about measures engaged. Almost without exception, CPs reserve the right to implement any subsequent lawful sanction of a general nature, in accordance with their own national legislation in force, in addition to applying disciplinary measures of the agreement itself (non-prejudice clause).

Concerning the obligation of the CPs to *exchange information* on the implementation of the agreement and related matters, an important number of agreements (26.3 percent) does not foresee such a duty at all.

Wherever this provision exists in the agreement, the following subjects have been identified for information exchange: accidents and other daily problems of transport operations (such as distress situations), statistics on the use of bilateral transport permits, traffic conditions, border crossing situations, and so forth. Only a handful of agreements require regular information exchange on possible changes in relevant national legislation.

Notes

1. For convenience, the short version of the parties' official country name is used throughout the study.
2. Customs Convention on the International Transport of Goods under Cover of TIR Carnets (TIR Convention); http://www.unece.org/tir/tirconv/conv75.html.
3. Vienna Convention on the Law of Treaties; http://treaties.un.org/Pages/ViewDetailsIII. aspx?&src=TREATY&mtdsg_no=XI-B-19&chapter=11&Temp=mtdsg3&lang=en.
4. Agreement on the International Carriage of Perishable Foodstuffs and on the Special Equipment to be Used for such Carriage; www.unece.org/trans/main/wp11/wp11fdoc/ATP-2007e.pdf.
5. Agreement Concerning the Work of Crews of Vehicles engaged in International Road Transport; http://treaties.un.org/Pages/ViewDetails.aspx?src=TREATY&mtdsg_no=XI-B-18&chapter=11&lang=en.
6. In figure 4.2 a "Yes" in case of triangular transport means the requirement for ordinary (regular) third-country transport permits, while "No" means either an open-ended regime or special permit or prohibition, while "No" for bilateral and transit transport means that no permits are required at all (open-ended operations).
7. http://treaties.un.org/pages/ViewDetails.aspx?src=TREATY&mtdsg_no=XI-A-17&chapter=11&lang=en.
8. http://www.unece.org/trans/conventn/legalinst_25_OLIRT_CMR.html.

CHAPTER 5

Findings on Bilateral Agreements

As explained above, an assessment was made of the features that help to quantify the degree of openness of bilateral road transport agreements. The scoring scheme presented in table 5.1 has proven effective in establishing the degree of openness of the agreements reviewed. Scoring was not possible for just one transit-only agreement, which was not comparable with the other documents.

In accordance with a decision reached by the Project Team, even if subtractive "penalty points" resulted in negative subtotals, these were retained, and the final total score of each agreement was calculated accordingly.

As detailed quantification results show, final total scores accumulate mainly in the middle ranks of the scale (according to the Gauss or bell curve). This is because, on the one hand, even the least open agreements contain sufficient positive elements not be scored too low or zero; and on the other hand, not even the most open agreements meet all highly demanding openness requirements of the 11 core features—for example, under the items facilitation and transparency. By allowing negative values, the weight of these two features grew compared to the original maximum of marks/weights (10 for Facilitation Measures and 7 for Transparency). These "soft" openness features and their forward-looking character allow precise expression of the lack of one or another useful openness component in the agreements.

The 77 agreements, ordered by degree of openness, are presented in figure 5.1. According to these results, the agreement between Tanzania and Zambia is the least open (20 points out of 100), whereas the agreement between Belarus and the Netherlands is the most open (83 points out of 100).

Standard deviation from the average of the whole population (47.59) is 15.35, while the distribution of analyzed agreements seems to be balanced towards the lower end, with the lowest and highest 25-point ranges containing only two and three agreements respectively. The majority of results (45–59.21 percent) fall between scores of 26 and 50. Within this category, most agreements (15) have an openness ranking between 36 and 40 points (figure 5.2). The median value for the 76 scores is 43.5.

Figure 5.1 Scoring Results of Assessed Agreements

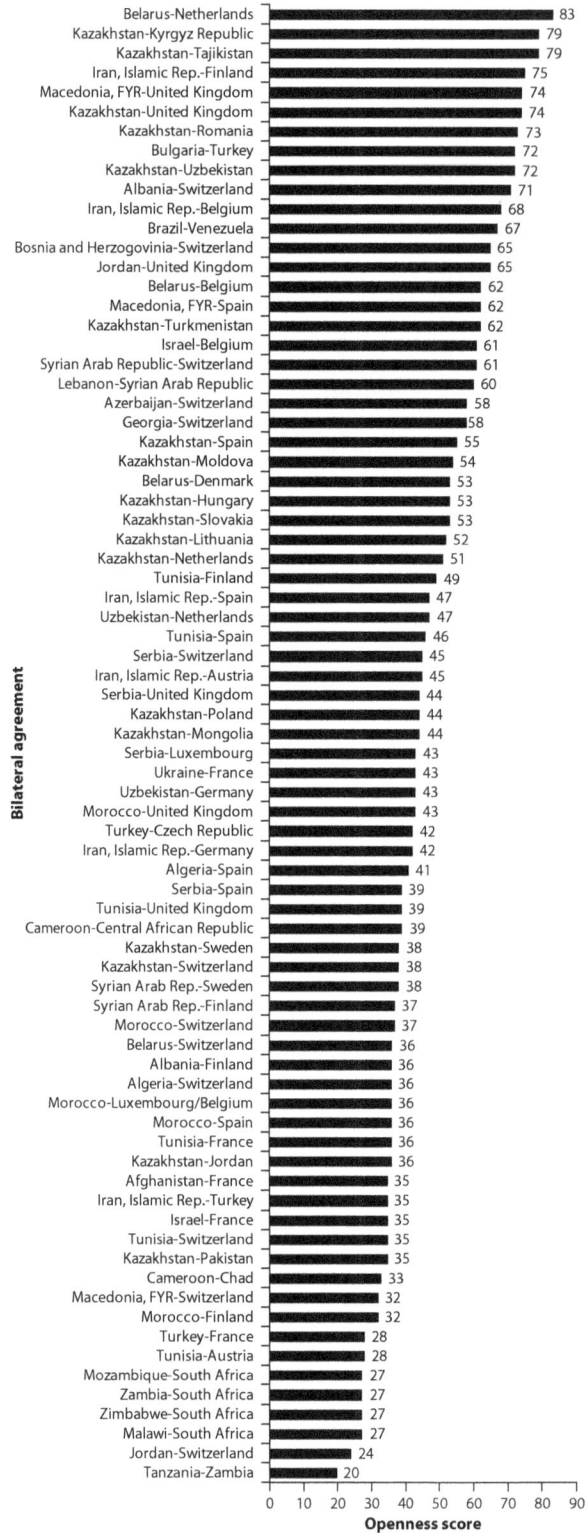

Bilateral agreement	Openness score
Belarus-Netherlands	83
Kazakhstan-Kyrgyz Republic	79
Kazakhstan-Tajikistan	79
Iran, Islamic Rep.-Finland	75
Macedonia, FYR-United Kingdom	74
Kazakhstan-United Kingdom	74
Kazakhstan-Romania	73
Bulgaria-Turkey	72
Kazakhstan-Uzbekistan	72
Albania-Switzerland	71
Iran, Islamic Rep.-Belgium	68
Brazil-Venezuela	67
Bosnia and Herzogovinia-Switzerland	65
Jordan-United Kingdom	65
Belarus-Belgium	62
Macedonia, FYR-Spain	62
Kazakhstan-Turkmenistan	62
Israel-Belgium	61
Syrian Arab Republic-Switzerland	61
Lebanon-Syrian Arab Republic	60
Azerbaijan-Switzerland	58
Georgia-Switzerland	58
Kazakhstan-Spain	55
Kazakhstan-Moldova	54
Belarus-Denmark	53
Kazakhstan-Hungary	53
Kazakhstan-Slovakia	53
Kazakhstan-Lithuania	52
Kazakhstan-Netherlands	51
Tunisia-Finland	49
Iran, Islamic Rep.-Spain	47
Uzbekistan-Netherlands	47
Tunisia-Spain	46
Serbia-Switzerland	45
Iran, Islamic Rep.-Austria	45
Serbia-United Kingdom	44
Kazakhstan-Poland	44
Kazakhstan-Mongolia	44
Serbia-Luxembourg	43
Ukraine-France	43
Uzbekistan-Germany	43
Morocco-United Kingdom	43
Turkey-Czech Republic	42
Iran, Islamic Rep.-Germany	42
Algeria-Spain	41
Serbia-Spain	39
Tunisia-United Kingdom	39
Cameroon-Central African Republic	39
Kazakhstan-Sweden	38
Kazakhstan-Switzerland	38
Syrian Arab Rep.-Sweden	38
Syrian Arab Rep.-Finland	37
Morocco-Switzerland	37
Belarus-Switzerland	36
Albania-Finland	36
Algeria-Switzerland	36
Morocco-Luxembourg/Belgium	36
Morocco-Spain	36
Tunisia-France	36
Kazakhstan-Jordan	36
Afghanistan-France	35
Iran, Islamic Rep.-Turkey	35
Israel-France	35
Tunisia-Switzerland	35
Kazakhstan-Pakistan	35
Cameroon-Chad	33
Macedonia, FYR-Switzerland	32
Morocco-Finland	32
Turkey-France	28
Tunisia-Austria	28
Mozambique-South Africa	27
Zambia-South Africa	27
Zimbabwe-South Africa	27
Malawi-South Africa	27
Jordan-Switzerland	24
Tanzania-Zambia	20

Source: World Bank data.

Figure 5.2 Distribution of Agreement Scores by Score Categories

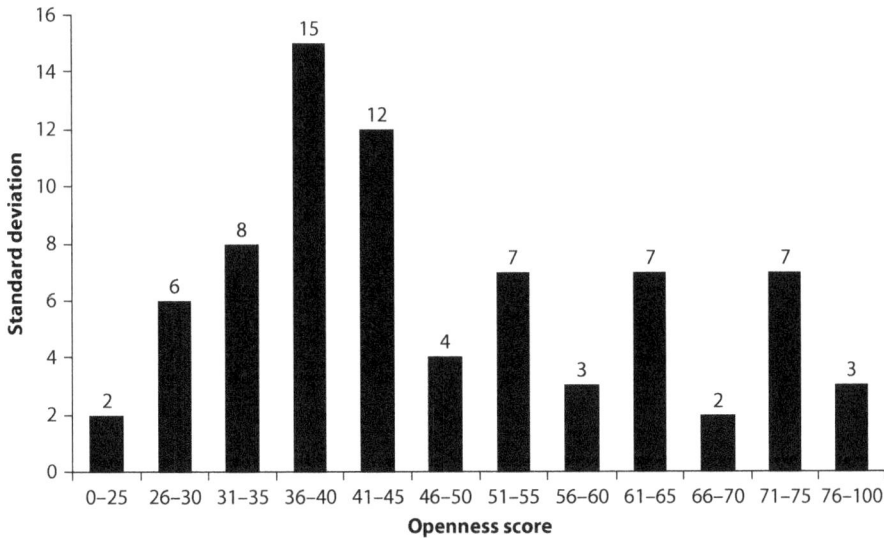

Source: World Bank data.

These results confirm that none of the agreements above the average openness score (30 agreements with an average score of 64.04 representing 39.47 percent of the 76 agreements) are close to the "ideal" 100 score—that is, the upper level benchmark requirements set in the Typology Questionnaire. On the lower end (46 agreements below average with an average score of 36.86 representing 60.52 percent of the 76 agreements), even the worst scores are well above zero.

In general, the 11 core features of the *top five agreements* are illustrated in table 5.1). Their average score is 78.

The 11 main features of the *five least open agreements* are presented in table 5.2. Their average score is 25.

This report studied the relationship between the degree of openness and the date of conclusion of agreements, looking in particular for signs that deregulation in the transport industry since the 1980s has had an impact on international agreements. It may be stated (agreements without a date of conclusion omitted) with some caution that after a decline period of 1971–80, the degree of openness of bilateral road transport agreements increased (figure 5.3).

This report also considered whether the degree of openness depended on the geographic relationship of agreements. For the agreements selected, it is evident that bilateral agreements signed between Asian countries have a higher level of openness than those concluded in other geographic relations. This high score (58 in average for 9 agreements) is due to the relatively open agreements signed between Kazakhstan and most of its neighbors. Agreements signed in Southern Africa seem to feature the lowest scores (29 in average for 7 agreements) due

Table 5.1 Eleven Core Features of Most Open Agreements

Agreement between		Score
Macedonia, FYR–United Kingdom		**74**
1. Limitations of scope (max 5)	One type of traffic prohibited	4
2. Transport permit requirements, permit management (max 15)	No permit requirement	15
3. Traffic exempted from permits (max 10)	No permit requirement	10
4. Traffic exempted from quotas (max 8)	No permit requirement, no quota	8
5. Cabotage traffic limitations (max 5)	Prohibited	3
6. Transit quota limitations (max 15)	No permit requirement	15
7. Triangular/third-country traffic limitations (max 9)	No permit requirement	9
8. Prescribed routes and border crossing points (max 8)	None	8
9. Taxation related limitations (max 8)	No fiscal preference for combined transport	6
10. Facilitation measures (max 10)	No international vehicle weight certificate; no international vehicle inspection certificate; no driving license clause; no clause on office establishment; no other facilitation measures	0
11. Transparency (max 7)	JC decisions not public; no appeal clause; no clause on information exchange; no clause of registration of agreement with UN Secretary General; no clause on access to national legislation; no clause on dispute settlement; no clause on amendment procedure	−4

Agreement between		Score
Islamic Republic of Iran–Finland		**75**
1. Limitations of scope (max 5)	One type of traffic prohibited	4
2. Transport permit requirements, permit management (max 15)	No permit, no quota	15
3. Traffic exempted from permits (max 10)	No permit, no quota	10
4. Traffic exempted from quotas (max 8)	No permit, no quota	8
5. Cabotage traffic limitations (max 5)	Prohibited	3
6. Transit quota limitations (max 15)	No permit, no quota	15
7. Triangular/third-country traffic limitations (max 9)	No permit, no quota	9
8. Prescribed routes and border crossing points (max 8)	None	8
9. Taxation related limitations (max 8)	No fiscal preference for combined transport	6
10. Facilitation measures (max 10)	No international vehicle weight certificate; no international vehicle inspection certificate; no driving license clause; no clause on office establishment; no other facilitation measures	0
11. Transparency (max 7)	JC decisions not public; no appeal clause; no clause on information exchange; no clause on access to national legislation; no clause on dispute settlement; no clause on amendment procedure	−3

(table continues on next page)

Table 5.1 Eleven Core Features of Most Open Agreements *(continued)*

Agreement between		Score
Kazakhstan-Tajikistan		**79**
1. Limitations of scope (max 5)	One type of traffic prohibited	4
2. Transport permit requirements, permit management (max 15)	No permit, no quota	15
3. Traffic exempted from permits (max 10)	No permit, no quota	10
4. Traffic exempted from quotas (max 8)	No permit, no quota	8
5. Cabotage traffic limitations (max 5)	Prohibited	3
6. Transit quota limitations (max 15)	No permit, no quota	15
7. Triangular/third-country traffic limitations (max 9)	No permit, no quota	9
8. Prescribed routes and border crossing points (max 8)	None	8
9. Taxation related limitations (max 8)	No fiscal preference for combined transport	6
10. Facilitation measures (max 10)	No international vehicle weight certificate; no international vehicle inspection certificate; no clause on office establishment; no clause on nondiscrimination	0
11. Transparency (max 7)	JC decisions not public; no appeal clause; no clause of registration of agreement with UN Secretary General	1

Agreement between		Score
Kazakhstan-Kyrgyz Republic		**79**
1. Limitations of scope (max 5)	One type of traffic prohibited	4
2. Transport permit requirements, permit management (max 15)	No permit, no quota	15
3. Traffic exempted from permits (max 10)	No permit, no quota	10
4. Traffic exempted from quotas (max 8)	No permit, no quota	8
5. Cabotage traffic limitations (max 5)	Prohibited	3
6. Transit quota limitations (max 15)	No permit, no quota	15
7. Triangular/third-country traffic limitations (max 9)	No permit, no quota	9
8. Prescribed routes and border crossing points (max 8)	None	8
9. Taxation related limitations (max 8)	No fiscal preference for combined transport	6
10. Facilitation measures (max 10)	No international vehicle weight certificate; no international vehicle inspection certificate; no clause on office establishment; no clause on nondiscrimination	0
11. Transparency (max 7)	JC decisions not public; no appeal clause; no clause of registration of agreement with UN Secretary General	1

Agreement between		Score
Belarus-The Netherlands		**83**
1. Limitations of scope (max 5)	No limitations	5
2. Transport permit requirements, permit management (max 15)	No quotas, just permits	15

(table continues on next page)

Table 5.1 Eleven Core Features of Most Open Agreements *(continued)*

		Score
3. Traffic exempted from permits (max 10)	Sufficient exemptions	10
4. Traffic exempted from quotas (max 8)	No quotas	8
5. Cabotage traffic limitations (max 5)	Allowed with special permit	4
6. Transit quota limitations (max 15)	No quotas	15
7. Triangular/third-country traffic limitations (max 9)	No quotas	9
8. Prescribed routes and border crossing points (max 8)	None	8
9. Taxation related limitations (max 8)	No fiscal preference for combined transport	6
10. Facilitation measures (max 10)	No International vehicle weight certificate; no vehicle technical inspection certificate; no driving license. clause; no clause on office establishment; no other facilitation measures	0
11. Transparency (max 7)	No appeal clause; no clause on registration with UN Secretary General; no dispute settlement clause	3

Source: World Bank data.
Note: JC = Joint committee.

Table 5.2 Eleven Main Features of Least Open Agreements

Agreement between		*Score*
Tanzania-Zambia		**20**
1. Limitations of scope (max 5)	Two types of traffic prohibited; special. authorization needed; permit validity less than six months	−1
2. Transport permit requirements, permit management (max 15)	Bilateral quota; quota approval time not fixed; no additional quota for modern vehicle/combined transport; double approval	4
3. Traffic exempted from permits (max 10)	No exemption list	4
4. Traffic exempted from quotas (max 8)	No exemption list	3
5. Cabotage traffic limitations (max 5)	Prohibited	3
6. Transit quota limitations (max 15)	Transit quota; no additional quota for modern vehicle/combined transport	6
7. Triangular/third-country traffic limitations (max 9)	Triangular quota; route restriction; no additional quota for modern vehicle/combined transport	2
8. Prescribed routes and border crossing points (max 8)	Route restriction; no roadside support services	0
9. Taxation related limitations (max 8)	No tax exemption; no fiscal preference for combined transport	0
10. Facilitation measures (max 10)	No clause on tractor and trailer registered in different countries; no clause on office establishment; no clause on nondiscrimination	−1
11. Transparency (max 7)	JC decisions not public; no appeal clause; no clause on registration with UN Secretary General; no clause on access to national legislation	0

(table continues on next page)

Table 5.2 Eleven Main Features of Least Open Agreements *(continued)*

		Score
Jordan-Switzerland		**24**
1. Limitations of scope (max 5)	One type of traffic prohibited	4
2. Transport permit requirements, permit management (max 15)	Bilateral quota; quota approval time not fixed; no additional quota for modern vehicle/combined transport	8
3. Traffic exempted from permits (max 10)	No exemption list	4
4. Traffic exempted from quotas (max 8)	No exemption list	3
5. Cabotage traffic limitations (max 5)	Prohibited	3
6. Transit quota limitations (max 15)	Transit quota; no additional quota for modern vehicle/combined transport	6
7. Triangular/third-country traffic limitations (max 9)	Triangular quota; route restriction; no additional quota for modern vehicle/combined transport	1
8. Prescribed routes and border crossing points (max 8)	None	8
9. Taxation related limitations (max 8)	No tax clause; no exemption for fuel in tanks; no fiscal preference for combined transport	−2
10. Facilitation measures (max 10)	No international vehicle weight certificate; no international vehicle inspection certificate; no clause on tractor and trailer registered in different countries; no driving license clause; no clause on nondiscrimination; no clause on office establishment; no other facilitation measure	−8
11. Transparency (max 7)	JC decisions not public; no appeal clause; no clause on exchange of information; no clause on registration with UN Secretary General; no clause on access to national legislation; no clause on amendment procedure	−3

Agreement between		Score
Malawi-South Africa		**27**
1. Limitations of scope (max 5)	Two types of traffic prohibited; permit validity less than six months; exclusivity applied	1
2. Transport permit requirements, permit management (max 15)	Bilateral quota; quota approval time not fixed; no additional quota for modern vehicle/combined transport; double approval	4
3. Traffic exempted from permits (max 10)	Less than 50% exemptions	6
4. Traffic exempted from quotas (max 8)	Less than 50% exemptions	5
5. Cabotage traffic limitations (max 5)	Prohibited	3
6. Transit quota limitations (max 15)	Transit quota; no additional quota for modern vehicle/combined transport	6
7. Triangular/third-country traffic limitations (max 9)	Forbidden	2
8. Prescribed routes and border crossing points (max 8)	Route restriction; no roadside support services	0
9. Taxation related limitations (max 8)	No tax clause; no duty exemption for fuel in tanks; no fiscal preference for combined transport	−2

(table continues on next page)

Table 5.2 Eleven Main Features of Least Open Agreements *(continued)*

		Score
10. Facilitation measures (max 10)	No clause on tractor and trailer registered in diff. countries; no clause on drivers license; no clause on office establishment;	2
11. Transparency (max 7)	JC decisions not public; no appeal clause; no clause on registration with UN Secretary General; no clause on access to national legislation	0

Agreement between		Score
Zimbabwe-South Africa		**27**
1. Limitations of scope (max 5)	Two types of traffic prohibited; permit validity less than six months; exclusivity applied	1
2. Transport permit requirements, permit management (max 15)	Bilateral quota; quota approval time not fixed; no additional quota for modern vehicle/combined transport; double approval	4
3. Traffic exempted from permits (max 10)	Less than 50% exemptions	6
4. Traffic exempted from quotas (max 8)	Less than 50% exemptions	5
5. Cabotage traffic limitations (max 5)	Prohibited	3
6. Transit quota limitations (max 15)	Transit quota; no additional quota for modern vehicle/combined transport	6
7. Triangular/third-country traffic limitations (max 9)	Forbidden	2
8. Prescribed routes and border crossing points (max 8)	Route restrictions; no roadside support services	0
9. Taxation related limitations (max 8)	No tax clause; no duty exemption for fuel in tanks; no fiscal preference for combined transport	−2
10. Facilitation measures (max 10)	No clause on tractor and trailer registered in different countries; no clause on drivers license; no clause on office establishment	2
11. Transparency (max 7)	JC decisions not public; no appeal clause; no clause on registration with UN Secretary General; no clause on access to national legislation	0

Agreement between		Score
Zambia-South Africa		**27**
1. Limitations of scope (max 5)	Two types of traffic prohibited; permit validity less than six months; exclusivity applied	1
2. Transport permit requirements, permit management (max 15)	Bilateral quota; quota approval time not fixed; no additional quota for modern vehicle/combined transport; double approval	4
3. Traffic exempted from permits (max 10)	Less than 50% exemptions	6
4. Traffic exempted from quotas (max 8)	Less than 50% exemptions	5
5. Cabotage traffic limitations (max 5)	Prohibited	3
6. Transit quota limitations (max 15)	Transit quota; no additional quota for modern vehicle/combined transport	6
7. Triangular/third-country traffic limitations (max 9)	Forbidden	2

(table continues on next page)

Table 5.2 Eleven Main Features of Least Open Agreements *(continued)*

		Score
8. Prescribed routes and border crossing points (max 8)	Route restriction; no roadside support services	0
9. Taxation related limitations (max 8)	No tax clause; no duty exemption for fuel in tanks; no fiscal preference for combined transport	−2
10. Facilitation measures (max 10)	No clause on tractor and trailer registered in different countries; no clause on drivers license; no clause on office establishment	2
11. Transparency (max 7)	JC decisions not public; no appeal clause; no clause on registration with UN Secretary General; no clause on access to national legislation	0

Source: World Bank data.
Note: JC = Joint committee.

Figure 5.3 Average Degree of Openness by Date of Conclusion of Agreements

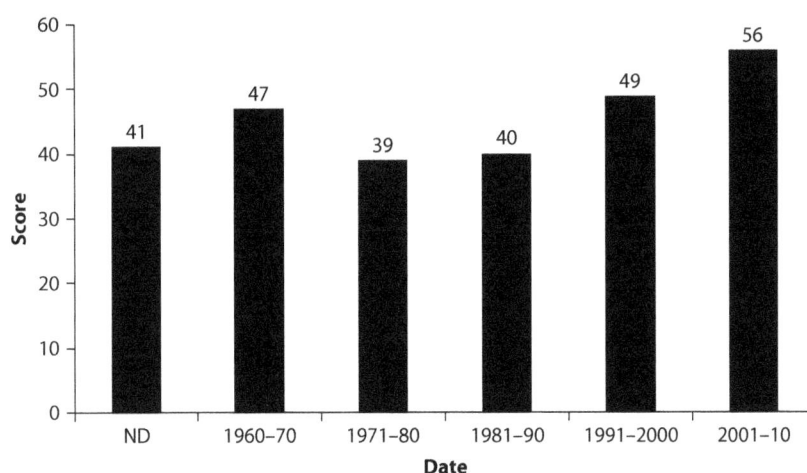

Source: World Bank data.
Note: Labels above bars show average scoring and the number of agreements concluded in the given period.
n.a. = Not applicable.

to "heavily sanctioned" restrictive provisions. They include several types of traffic prohibited, double approval procedure applied for permits and quotas, exclusivity applied to carriers and vehicles of the two CPs only, less than 50 percent of items on the standard cargo list exempted from permits and quotas, route restrictions (and no roadside support services), no tax clause, no duty exemption for fuel in tanks, and so forth. Drafting bilateral agreements in this region has certainly been influenced by the model bilateral agreement signed on a multilateral basis by countries of the Southern Africa region.

Agreements concluded between Northern Africa and European states seem also to be relatively restrictive (38 in average for 13 agreements) (figure 5.4).

Figure 5.4 Average Openness of Agreements by Geographic Relations

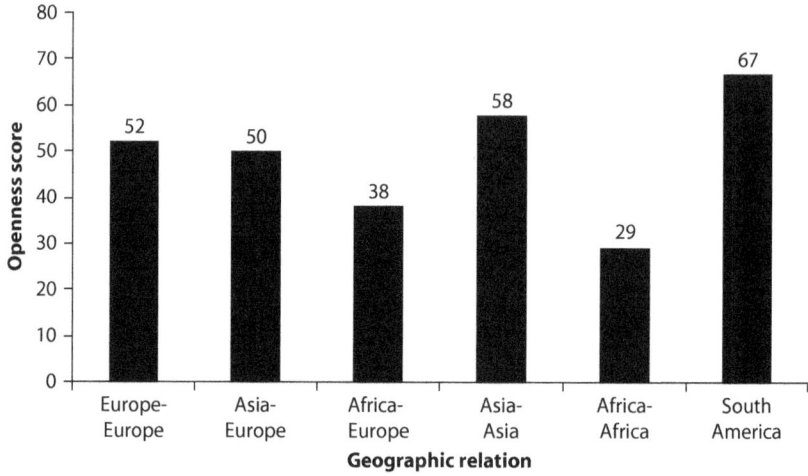

Source: World Bank data.
Note: Labels above bars show average scoring/number of agreements concluded in the given geographic relation.

Figure 5.5 Scores for Agreements between Kazakhstan and Different Parties

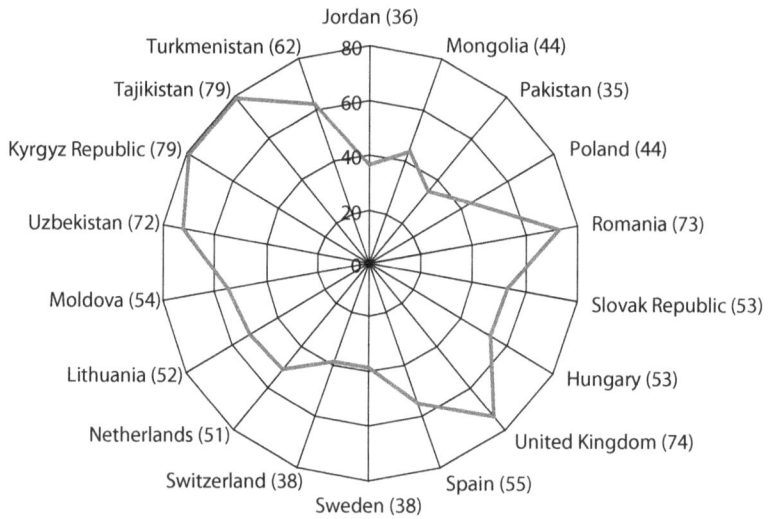

Source: World Bank data.

Another striking feature is that the agreements signed by one country with different partners all tend to be different. For instance, Kazakhstan had 18 agreements in the sample but its scores ranged from 35 with Pakistan to a high of 79 with the Kyrgyz Republic. Figure 5.5 shows the scores of Kazakhstan's agreements with different parties.

CHAPTER 6

Findings on Multilateral Agreements

Bilateral agreements are certainly influenced by multilateral ones to which most bilateral contracting parties (CPs) in a region concerned are simultaneously signatories. We characterized the features of this interrelationship in table 6.1, where eight intraregional, multilateral agreements are listed. These agreements were reviewed and ranked using the same ranking methodology as that used for reviewing bilateral documents.

At a later stage, consideration may be given to developing a special typology for benchmarking the openness of intraregional multilateral agreements, which are far from being homogeneous.

Table 6.1 Scoring of Intraregional, Multilateral Agreements and Models

Geographic region	Agreement/MoU/model title	Scores
Europe	Recommended Model Bilateral Agreement on Road Transport between ECMT Member Countries	57
	South-East European Cooperation Initiative (SECI) Memorandum of Understanding on the Facilitation of International Road Transport of Goods	59
Black Sea Region	Memorandum of Understanding on Facilitation of Road Transport of Goods in the BSEC Region and (together with) Black Sea Economic Cooperation (BSEC) Agreement on Multilateral Transit Permits	40
Asia (South-East Asia)	Agreement between and among the Governments of the Lao People's Democratic Republic, the Kingdom of Thailand, and the Socialist Republic of Vietnam for Facilitation of Cross-Border Transport of Goods and People (Cross-Border Transport Agreement [CBTA])	75
Africa	Memorandum of Understanding on Road Transportation in the Common Customs Area pursuant to the Customs Union Agreement between the Governments of Botswana, Lesotho, South Africa, and Swaziland (SACU MoU)	46
	SATCC Model Bilateral Agreement on the Regulation of Cross-Border Freight Road Transport	25
	Tripartite Agreement on Road Transport Uganda-Kenya-Tanzania	40
South America	Agreement on International Land Transport (Latin American Integration Association [ALADI])	56

Source: World Bank data.

Memorandum types of documents include the Memorandum of Understanding (MoU), examples of which are taken from the South-East European Cooperation Initiative (SECI) and the Black Sea Economic Cooperation (BSEC). MoUs are rather loose compendia of goodwill declarations that in principle should be given a step-by-step follow-up among signatories in further specific multilateral or bilateral agreements. The BSEC MoU has already been complemented by a specific BSEC Agreement on Multilateral Transit Permits, and this document has indeed been considered together with the region's MoU for benchmarking purposes.

Exception to the mainly general character of MoUs is the MoU on road transportation in the South African Customs Union (SACU), which is rather detailed and practical. For example, the MoU defines a phasing-in process of quota development whereby market shares of operators registered in territories of different pairs of CPs move from imbalanced toward balanced. In practice, issues covered by this multilateral agreement are tackled in a series of bilateral agreements.

Template bilateral agreements are compilations of legal solutions to intrare-gional multilateral issues that have been or are likely to be implemented in countries of the region concerned. Examples are the model bilateral agree-ments of the Southern African Transport and Communication Commission (SATCC) or the European Conference of Ministers of Transport (ECMT). These template agreements are not necessarily the most "progressive" solutions, but rather are harmonization-minded groupings of provisions that can be accepted by most countries. ECMT has enacted an interesting system, whereby the recommended bilateral model is indirectly supported by a highly progressive and efficient multilateral permit and quota system (a real alternative to bilaterally reciprocal rigidities). The system allows free access to bilateral, transit, and third-country transport market segments for transport companies and their vehicles registered in the territory of an ECMT member state. For decades, the flexible ECMT regime has functioned successfully and supported economic development in Europe. Recently, however, the system has suffered a serious setback due to the introduction of various uni-lateral or jointly agreed restrictions on previously guaranteed freedoms. These new restrictions are a response to developments such as the enlargement of the European Union (EU) and the protracted global economic-financial crisis (box 6.1).

The situation is explained by the International Transport Forum (ITF) as follows: "The fundamental aim of the ECMT System is to gradually liberalize international markets at a high level of quality. However the ability of the current System to achieve that aim has been reduced due to a range of geo-political and economic factors. In recent years, there has been very little political support for liberalization measures and some Countries have become more protectionist, an attitude undoubtedly reinforced by the recent economic crisis" (ITF 2011).

Box 6.1

ECMT Multilateral Quota System

The text below uses extracts from ITF documents to describe the ECMT Multilateral Quota System.

From the "Report of the High Level Group for the Development of the Multilateral Quota System" (ITF 2011):

"The ECMT Multilateral Quota System has been operating since January 1974 with the aim of both facilitating trade and improving efficiency in the international road freight transport market. It has developed over the years, responding to both changes in membership and transport policies, with membership more than doubling in the 1990s to over 40 countries. It has responded to growing concerns about the environment in its development of the green lorry concept with the overall aim of making the System a symbol of the highest quality in international transport.

The System provides a multilateral complement to bilateral agreements. Multilateralism facilitates the realization of the economic benefits of opening international markets and the ECMT System is a stepping stone in this direction. It is seen as a way to improve quality in the sector and open markets at the same time."

From the *ECMT Multilateral Quota User Guide* (ITF 2009):

"ECMT licenses are multilateral licenses for the international carriage of goods by road for hire or reward by transport undertakings established in an ECMT Member country, on the basis of a quota system, the transport operations being performed:

- Between ECMT Member countries and
- In transit through the territory of one or several ECMT Member country(ies) by vehicles registered in an ECMT Member country.

The licenses are not valid for transport operations between a Member and a non-member country. There are annual and short-term licenses.

ECMT licenses are issued, depending on national criteria, to road transport undertakings duly authorized to operate by the competent Authority of the country in which they are established. ECMT Member countries recognize the validity of licenses issued by another Member country.

When a journey is undertaken using a coupled combination of vehicles, the license is obtained from the competent Authority in the country in which the tractor is registered. This license covers the coupled combination of vehicles, even if the trailer or the semi-trailer is not registered in the name of the holder of the license, or is registered in another Member country.

The country of loading of the vehicle may be different of the country of origin of the goods loaded. An ECMT license does not authorize cabotage. An ECMT license may be used for vehicles hired or leased, without a driver, by the transport undertaking to which it has been issued."

Sources: ITF 2009, 2011.

The third category of intraregional, multilateral documents is represented by specific agreements on international road transport. Examples of the category include the following:

- Agreement between and among the governments of the Lao People's Democratic Republic, the Kingdom of Thailand, and the Socialist Republic of Vietnam for Facilitation of Cross-Border Transport of Goods and People (Cross-Border Transport Agreement [CBTA])
- Tripartite Agreement on Road Transport Uganda-Kenya-Tanzania
- Agreement on International Land Transport (Latin American Integration Association [ALADI]).

Without judging their success and efficiency in practice, these agreements contain the most pragmatic legal provisions for a limited number of signatory states. They are applicable without the need to be transformed into further international (for example, bilateral) agreements or reiterated by national legislation.

Table 6.1 illustrates the results of the intraregional, multilateral scoring exercise.

The low score obtained by the SATCC Model Bilateral Agreement is the consequence of significant restrictions contained therein: permits for bilateral and transit operations, permit quotas, double approval of permits/quotas, limited number of exemptions from permits/quotas, prohibition of cabotage and third-country transports, route restrictions, no tax and customs duty exemptions, and lack of sufficient facilitation and transparency provisions.

At the other extremity of the scale, the high score of the trilateral CBTA is mainly due to the "no-permit regime." This regime automatically prohibits quotas for any type of operation with the exception of cabotage, no route restrictions, at least partial tax exemption, and a number of agreed facilitation and transparency measures.

By comparing the scores of the multilateral and the bilateral agreements for the same geographic relations/regions, an interrelationship between their scores can be discerned. The openness of bilateral and multilateral schemes are relatively close in the same region, as shown in table 6.2 and figure 6.1.[1]

Of course, the sample analyzed may not be sufficient for a valid conclusion. It opens a door, however, for further qualitative deliberations and comparisons between the two schemes, which could help deepen the existing knowledge in this respect.

Before leaving the question of multilateral agreements, one should remember the importance of a multitude of multilateral regulations that influence the functioning of either bilateral or intraregional regulatory arrangements of international road transport. Emphasis is put in this study on legal frameworks that overarch national and/or regional frontiers, such as UN or other international agreements and conventions. Many of these have been referenced in a number

Table 6.2 Ranking Comparison of Multilateral and Bilateral Agreements

Intraregional multilateral agreement	Multilateral score	Average bilateral score
SATCC Model Bilateral Agreement on the Regulation of Cross-Border Freight Road Transport	25	29[a]
Memorandum of Understanding on Facilitation of Road Transport of Goods in the BSEC Region and (together with) Black Sea Economic Cooperation (BSEC) Agreement on Multilateral Transit Permits	40	50[b]
Tripartite Agreement on Road Transport Uganda-Kenya-Tanzania	40	—
Memorandum of Understanding on Road Transportation in the Common Customs Area pursuant to the Customs Union Agreement between the Governments of Botswana, Lesotho, South Africa, and Swaziland (SACU MoU)	46	29[c]
Agreement on International Land Transport (Latin American Integration Association [ALADI])	56	67[d]
Recommended Model Bilateral Agreement on Road Transport between ECMT Member Countries	57	52[e], 50[f]
South-East European Cooperation Initiative (SECI) Memorandum of Understanding on the Facilitation of International Road Transport of Goods	59	52[g]
Agreement between and among the Governments of the Lao People's Democratic Republic, the Kingdom of Thailand, and the Socialist Republic of Vietnam for Facilitation of Cross-Border Transport of Goods and People (Cross-Border Transport Agreement [CBTA])	75	58[h]

Source: World Bank data.
Notes: — = Not available.
a. Average score of Africa-Africa bilateral agreements.
b. Average score of Asia-Europe bilateral agreements.
c. Average score of Africa-Africa bilateral agreements.
d. Agreement between Brazil and República Bolivariana de Venezuela.
e. Average score of Europe-Europe bilateral agreements.
f. Average score of Asia-Europe bilateral agreements.
g. Average score of Europe-Europe bilateral agreements.
h. No bilateral agreements have been reviewed for the region; the closest is the average score of Asia-Asia bilateral agreements.

of bilateral agreements as mentioned earlier, like the Customs Convention on the International Transport of Goods under Cover of TIR Carnets (TIR Convention) or the European Agreement concerning the International Carriage of Dangerous Goods by Road (ADR), the Agreement on the International Carriage of Perishable Foodstuffs and on the Special Equipment to be Used for such Carriage (ATP), the Agreement Concerning the Work of Crews of Vehicles engaged in International Road Transport (AETR) agreement on driving and rest time rules and the application of the related on-board checking equipment (tachograph). Also important are pieces of EU legislation that have mandatory application to "visiting" transport operators registered in third-countries and operating in EU territory on the basis of bilateral agreements in geo-relations like Asia-Europe or Africa-Europe. Further multilateral transport instruments of high relevance include the Convention on the Contract for the International

Figure 6.1 Ranking Comparison of Multilateral and Bilateral Agreements

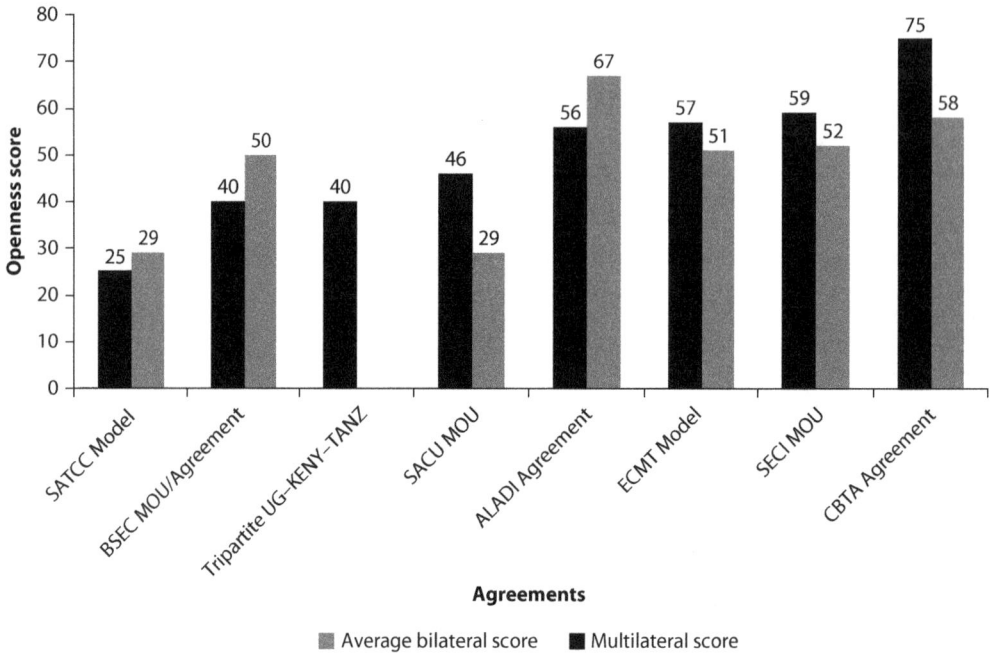

SATCC - Southern African Transport Communications Commission
BSEC   - Black Sea Economic Cooperation
MOU   - Memorandum of Understanding
ALADI - Latin American Integration Association
ECMT   - European Conference of Ministers of Transport
SECI   - South-East European Cooperation Initiative
CBTA   - Cross-Border Transport Agreement

Source: World Bank data.

Carriage of Goods by Road (CMR), conventions on road infrastructure development, road traffic safety, vehicle technical requirements, facilitation of border
crossing, dangerous and perishable goods transport, the General Agreement on
Tariffs and Trade (GATT) and General Agreement on Trade in Services (GATS),
and so forth.

Note

1. This initial observation is completely different from experience of the air transport
agreements (see Quantitative Air Services Agreement Review [QUASAR] of World
Trade Organization [WTO]), where the openness level of multilateral agreements
(though not fully applied) is twice as high as bilateral agreements in the same geographic relation (*Source:* Air Transport Agreement between the EU and Switzerland,
WTO, S/C/W/270/Add.2).

CHAPTER 7

Economic Importance of Agreements

Transport as a derived demand is generally reflective of the economic or social interactions between regions and countries. The analysis was therefore extended to assess whether there is a relationship between the degree of openness of agreements and the economic ties between the two parties. The work was based on identifying the macroeconomic importance of bilateral road transport agreements—for example answering the question whether road freight transport reflects an underlying demand for the movement of trade traffic.

A profound statistical analysis to determine the economic importance of agreements on the basis of bilateral road transport data would go beyond the scope of the present study. *Road freight traffic data* alone, if available, would have been sufficient and best suited for such an analysis as stated above. Ideally, this exercise should be based on origin-destination data. In the absence of such data the assessment relied on proxies. Three such proxies were used: (1) adjacency and proximity of the countries that are party to an agreement, (2) the size of the trucking fleets in the countries, and (3) the volume of international trade between the countries. The relationship between the degree of openness of the agreements and each of these factors was assessed first followed by a composite assessment. This analysis is only exploratory and the results are tentative and would require a more robust analytical approach.

Spatial Proximity of Contracting Parties

Compared with maritime shipping, road and rail are currently transporting relatively small quantities of internationally traded freight, particularly between different continents. Less than one quarter of global trade (measured in value) takes place between countries sharing a land border, where surface modes are assumed to be dominant (OECD 2010; WTO 2010). However, as land-based transport has a relative advantage in terms of cost per transit-time compared to water and air transport, its share in international shipping is expected to increase. Therefore, neighboring countries are likely to regulate their access to each other's market through bilateral agreements. However, based on the

Table 7.1 Distribution of Analyzed Agreements by Real Distance Categories

Kilometers travelled	Number of agreements
less than 1,000 km	11
1,001–1,499	15
1,500–2,000	11
2,001–3,000	10
3,001–3,500	13
More than 3,501	17

Source: World Bank data.

sample analyzed, no relation could be identified between the proximity of countries and the degree of openness of the agreements (table 7.1).

Spatial proximity has always been central to trade flow modeling, especially the quality and cost of moving between any two places. In this respect, the present study assessed the adjacency of countries that are party to an agreement measured in terms of the distance between capital cities. We corrected for topographic effects such as natural barriers like water bodies or high mountains, as well as the number of transit countries to travel through to reach the other country.

For the reviewed bilateral agreements, distances are understandably shortest in Europe-Europe geographic relations, while those in Asia-Europe are the longest. Generally, however it would appear that the longer the distance, the less important is the bilateral transport agreement from an economic point of view. This finding is consistent with observed average road freight transport distances in the European Union (EU) (figure 7.1). In the EU, 96 percent of all tonnages transported by road are moved on a distance shorter than 500 kilometers (domestic and international movements included).

Figure 7.1 Average Transport Distance, Total Road Transport, EU, 2008

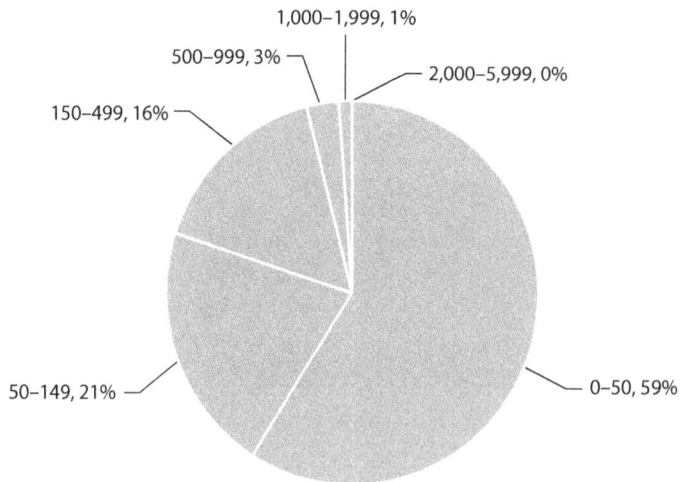

Source: http://appsso.eurostat.ec.europa.eu.

An additional hypothesis was also tested, namely that the longer the distance the more open the bilateral agreement of the pair of countries concerned. The idea is that contracting parties (CPs) of two distant countries sign bilateral road transport agreements for reinforcing their general economic, political, and diplomatic ties, rather than supporting and facilitating international freight movement by road, which is anyhow quantitatively insignificant due to distance. Competition between their haulers is certainly limited by the lack of geographic separation; therefore CPs may be more tolerant and less restrictive when drafting provisions of their agreement.

It was determined that about 50 percent of the agreements reviewed (those covering distances less than 2,000 kilometers) are more or less of sufficient distance where international road freight transport may play a meaningful role in carrying foreign trade goods to their destination. It is general experience that above distances of 2,000 kilometers (or even less), the longer the distance to cover, the more the trucking industry should specialize for niche markets (U.S. Chamber of Commerce 2006), like moving high-value or time-sensitive cargo.

Openness and Size of Bilateral Trade Flows

The study explored a possible link between the size of the bilateral trade flows between countries having road freight transport agreements and the degree of openness of such agreements. The assumption that was made was that the bigger the volume of demand between any pair of countries, the less concern about protecting access to the road freight market.

Not all trade traffic moves by road; in fact, the bulk of it, especially between coastal countries, moves by sea. The results suggest that there is no clear relationship between bilateral trade volume and openness. In fact, the trend based on the limited sample analyzed is slightly downwards (figure 7.2). Countries with large volumes of bilateral trade seem to have less open agreements than those that have lesser volumes. This can be explained by the earlier pattern identified above: less than 25 percent of global trade takes place between neighboring countries, where road transport would be expected to play a big role. In addition, there are pairs of countries that have agreements although the trade between them is very limited. Such countries would likely have concluded agreements for reasons other than economic ones, as described in chapter 2. If such is the case, then it is likely that any high transport costs between countries having bilateral road transport agreements and low trade volumes are not due to market access restrictions but to other factors, including, for instance, operational practices of incumbents.

Openness and Fleet Size

An attempt was made also to understand the extent to which the openness of agreements is related to the size of the trucking fleets in the partner countries (appendix C). An underlying assumption was that the larger the national

Figure 7.2 Volume of Bilateral Trade and Openness of Agreements

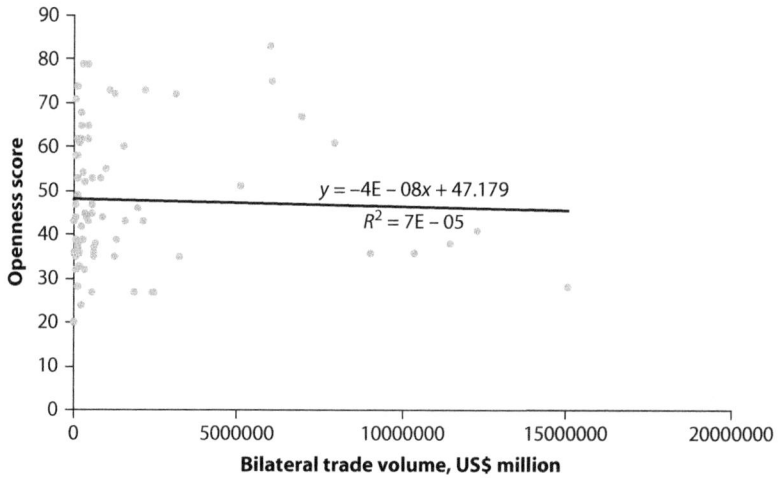

Source: World Bank data.

trucking fleet in each country, the more important would be the road freight agreements. It was assumed also that when the domestic market has a large fleet, it will likely be very competitive, in which case the impact of foreign players accessing the same market would be limited.

Based on the sample, there are few leading pairs of countries that have large fleets especially in the EU: they include countries like France, Spain, the United Kingdom, and Germany. The country pair Turkey-France takes the top position because of the large size of the Turkish truck fleet. National fleet sizes are more balanced in the middle range. Further refinement of these absolute figures was not attempted but deserves consideration through the application of specific data. For example, the number of trucks could be divided by the size of population, the surface of the country of vehicle registration, the size of the gross domestic product (GDP) of the home country, and/or the size of international and domestic fleets. A distinction between hire-and-reward and own-account fleets would also be beneficial.

Similar to the findings of the assessment of openness based on trade volume, the size of the fleet also has a slightly downward sloping relationship with openness (figure 7.3). Even controlling for whether or not one of the parties to an agreement is landlocked, this did not alter the general trend. There are two possible explanations for this tendency. First, in countries with large fleets, the trucking industry tends to be better organized and therefore able to lobby the governments and influence the content of agreements. It is common practice for road transport industry representatives to form part of the country delegations to negotiations of bilateral agreements, and they are notably present in the joint committee (JC) meetings, where the number of permits are decided. Second, in some countries the regulations can restrict the number of transport operators

Figure 7.3 Size of Trucking Fleet and Openness of Agreements

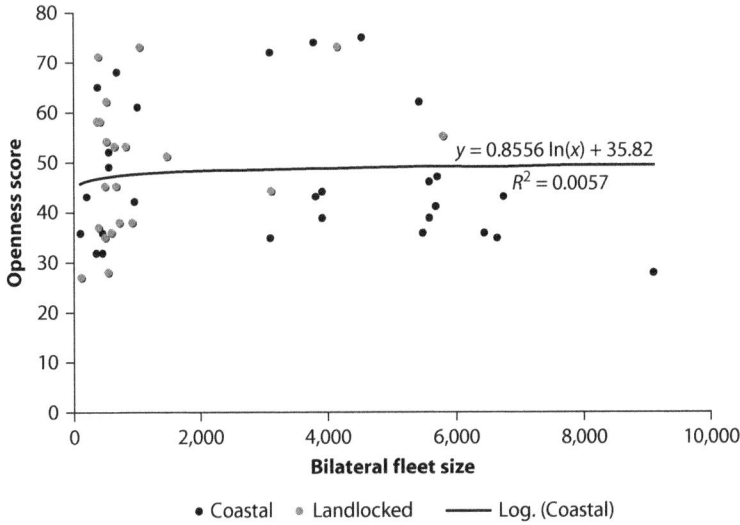

$y = 0.8556 \ln(x) + 35.82$

$R^2 = 0.0057$

● Coastal   ● Landlocked   —— Log. (Coastal)

Source: World Bank data.

that are authorized to perform international operations. Alternatively, the transport operators themselves specialize or focus on either domestic or cross-border road freight transport operations. In such cases the domestic truck fleet could be large, but the size of the fleet and number of operators involved in cross-border operations could be relatively small. As a result, such operators are still able to influence the content and coverage of bilateral agreements. The road freight transport sector is surrounded by significant political economy issues, particularly in low- and middle-income countries, an aspect that is usually reflected in the degree of openness of bilateral agreements.

The assessment of economic importance of agreements attempted here was only tentative. However, it confirmed that bilateral road freight transport agreements are not always concluded for their economic importance in facilitating bilateral trade flows. Political or other considerations for concluding such agreements are a reality, remain relevant, and should be analyzed when trying to understand why each agreement might have been concluded.

CHAPTER 8

Summary and Conclusions

Road freight transport plays an indispensable role among transport modes in ensuring mobility of people and the conduct of international economic cooperation and foreign trade. On a number of continents and land masses, its share is predominant, particularly for short and medium distances. Road transport also has proved to be vital on long-distance niche markets of international freight transport. Therefore, efforts should be made to minimize any physical or administrative barriers hampering smooth international road transport, notably for freight as an integral part of the trade logistics industry.

This study was motivated primarily by a realization that bilateral agreements are the main instrument used to govern and regulate international road transport services. Yet at the same time there is a general sense that the nature and content of such agreements is not always well known. Nor are the agreements readily accessible, especially among the community of service providers who are supposed to be the primary beneficiaries. As a result, it is not unusual for road transport service providers not to be fully aware of the provisions of the agreements or to take full advantage of their provisions. The study has confirmed some initial assumptions and has identified a few other patterns that are important to how countries and the development agencies that support them should approach regional road transport market integration and reforms. Ultimately, of course, bilateral agreements can either be building blocks to broader regional cooperation or they can become a major impediment. Some of the salient findings of the study are summarized below, starting with the general findings followed by some specific recommendations.

General Findings and Recommendations

There are numerous bilateral agreements with no apparent patterns to their content. The study confirmed two very important details. First, there are obviously numerous bilateral agreements between countries, but in most regions the majority of their texts are not readily available. This is a great disservice to the intended beneficiaries of the agreements as well as to the enforcement authorities, because compliance is not easy or opportunities remain unexploited if the agreements are not well known. Second, agreements between one country and any other two parties are not always the same. Depending on the political, economic, or other objectives of concluding the agreements, the scope and openness of any two agreements can be different. Countries will seek to balance their interests in any bilateral relationship, but this has consequences for service providers. Where requirements for entry into the international road transport sector or for compliance are different, this compromises the ability of service providers to optimize their operations and to minimize costs.

Model agreements need to be clear on their objective and limits. In some regions there have been attempts to encourage similarities between agreements by offering model agreements that countries could base their bilateral agreements on. The regional model agreements have been used to try and lay the ground for eventual convergence and regional road freight transport market integration. This has been the case under the European Conference of Ministers of Transport (ECMT) and in Southern Africa under Southern African Development Community (SADC). However, both models have limitations that are replicated in subsequent numerous bilateral agreements based on them. This is most apparent in the case of Southern Africa, where the SADC model has resulted in numerous bilateral agreements that are missing several elements, resulting in low degrees of openness. In order to be useful and progressive, model agreements should be clear on their scope and at best should only serve as a minimum that pairs of countries would be expected to exceed in their bilateral agreements. The intention in SADC was for the bilateral agreements to lay the ground for convergence and eventually lead to a multilateral agreement. However, this has not happened because the jump from the protections embedded in the bilateral schemes to a more permissive multilateral agreement would be too large for some countries. Under these circumstances, it might be more beneficial to define a new model that incorporates options and paths to convergence, so countries know the consequences of each restriction they may impose/accept and could agree to introduce in their bilateral negotiations.

There is no overarching international template for bilateral road transport agreements. One of the reasons why the quality of model bilateral agreements tends to vary is the absence of a widely applicable international template. Unlike bilateral agreements in air transport where partners can be anywhere in the globe, bilateral agreements on road transport tend to be more dependent on geography. As a result, the content and scope of agreements with any one country will have an impact on the potential for regional integration in the immediate neighborhood. One of the fascinating findings of the study, but one which still needs further verification, is that countries are more likely to negotiate more open bilateral agreements if their economic importance is less significant. If the main objective of the agreement is political, then this is intended to send certain signals and would not be primarily about transport efficiency. Unfortunately, the reasons for negotiating any agreement are not always apparent, especially when they lie outside the transport arena.

Assessing the extent of implementation of bilateral agreements is difficult. An agreement between any two parties is only as good as the extent of its implementation and enforcement. Ratifying an international legal instrument and concluding a bilateral agreement are very positive and relatively simple steps, but effective implementation is paramount to trade and transport facilitation. Becoming party to international legal instruments is a serious matter that requires careful analysis and evaluation at national level. This process may call for adaptation of national laws and institutions, the adoption of new technical standards in transport infrastructure and equipment, as well as acceptance of new organizational and operational systems. The legal instrument has thus to be evaluated to determine its benefits and implications for the government and the industry, as well as its overall economic, social, and financial impact. Ideally, the assessment of the degree of implementation should be based on documented comparison of legislations, but in most of the cases time and resource constraints impose simpler solutions. One of the possible solutions is to ask specific questions about the key provisions of each agreement. It is not always clear which offers more benefits: a restrictive agreement that is properly implemented or an open one that is poorly implemented and enforced. No measure has negligible impacts as long as it is intended to improve the operating environment.

Analysis of bilateral agreements can follow a systematic methodology. One of the major weaknesses in attempts to assist with reforms and transformation of international road transport services has been the lack of a tool to help guide analysis of current instruments. The methodology followed in this work has shown that it is feasible to execute a systematic assessment of such agreements. The approach utilizes a quantitative approach that has been used in similar exercises, including in the legal arena. A quantitative approach enables us to attempt comparisons of agreements as well as international benchmarking. The typology questionnaire developed as part of the present study proved highly effective in analyzing agreements from different parts of the world and in generating results that help focus attention on several key attributes of each agreement. The model can be used to assess a single agreement as part of the design of trade facilitation or transport projects.

Specific Findings and Recommendations

Countries should conclude, streamline, and implement transparent road transport agreements. Ever since the birth of international road freight transport activities, bilateral governmental regulation has proven to be a very efficient form of setting their general framework conditions. It is recalled that provided there is no efficient multilateral scheme in place and truly implemented among cooperating countries, bilateral agreements still play a major regulatory role.

Fundamental conditions of access to the international freight transport market have traditionally been the main subject of regulation through bilateral agreements. They cover issues like the application (or not) of preconditions of engaging in international operations (access to the profession), transport permits, and permit quotas, as well as more specific matters such as conditions of cabotage, transit and third-country operations, security and road safety, taxes, prescribed routes, facilitation measures, and so on. It is therefore recommended that countries should check the state of regulation of international road freight transport with their trade partners and conclude new or review already existing bilateral agreements. The goal should be to cover the widest possible scope of regulatory matters, while keeping in the forefront the joint interest of facilitating border-crossing road freight transport operations. Concerning transparency and availability, there are two common and efficient solutions: (1) publish the texts of the treaties to which a country is a contracting party (CP) in the national official journals, and (2) give the private sector responsibility for the knowledge platform. The latter practice is widely implemented in Europe, where professional associations of road transport operators are managing comprehensive agreement databases and providing access to their texts to members or stakeholders at large.

Emphasize qualitative over quantitative and multilateral over bilateral regulation. Worldwide experience has proven that strictly implemented, international, qualitative regulation of access-to-the-market conditions has many benefits. They include more competition on freight transport markets; better international logistics and supply chain service quality; improved trade and international production schemes, thanks to better delivery scheduling; and enhanced freight rate competitiveness based on diminishing transport costs. Examples of such regulation, which should replace previous quantitative restrictions of market access, include forward-looking requirements for access to the profession, for road safety, security, and protection of the environment.

Historically, it has been bilateral regulation that has greatly contributed to the development of a flourishing international freight transport industry. More recently, it has became evident that multilateral agreements, provided that authorities and operators respect and comply with them, offer smoother and more easily applicable conditions in a wider geographic area than that covered by specific bilateral regimes. However, a phased-out process of transition from bilateral towards multilateral schemes is essential to avoid harmful shocks to the established culture of transport and logistics operators and the industries they work for.

Countries should follow a step-by-step opening of their bilateral road transport agreements, and turn them into truly qualitative bilateral and later on multilateral regulatory tools. In doing so, they may want to draw on the conclusions of the present study and use it as a basic agreement benchmarking tool. The benchmarking tool in the form of the Typology Questionnaire represents an important but partial contribution to a planned World Bank Toolkit for Road Transport Sector Reform.

Adopt the principle of freedoms. An essential part of a qualitative regulatory scheme is the strong application of the principles of "freedoms". In the widest sense, they cover free trade in transport services; the seamless transfer of capital, setting up transport companies abroad; the smooth movement of carried goods across frontiers; and the application of most favored nation (MFN) as well as national treatment (NT) standards to the benefit of carriers engaged in international operations, and therefore, indirectly, trade operators.

Furthermore, multilateral agreements that substantially apply the freedom principles have proven to be the best means of harmonizing international regulations, particularly when compared to the intrinsically discriminating, highly heterogeneous, and segmented bilateral legal instruments. Countries should consider introducing the freedom principles into their existing or future bilateral agreements, and preferably into existing and future multilateral regulatory schemes of international road freight transport.

Simplify technical requirements. Advantages of the most flexible market access conditions can be wiped away by overregulated technical conditions of transport operations. Overregulation may involve vehicle technical standards, documentation and inspection, particular and unreasonable requirements for driver competences and licenses, and the obligation to provide special certificates for the cargo carried or other aspects of operations. Governments are advised to draw on existing technical requirements for the vehicle, driver, and cargo and to simplify technical documentation requirements. They should apply self-restrain by not inventing new technical, inspection-related, and other documentary requirements for international haulage.

Set transparent rules for horizontal issues. International freight transport operations are greatly affected by general policies pursued by governments in areas like visa issuance; security rules; and insurance regulation concerning the driver, the transport operator, the vehicle, the cargo, and specific transport operations. Furthermore, exemptions (or lack of) from visa obligations for professional drivers affects international transport efficiency and organization.

International transport security requirements should encompass existing legal instruments. These instruments include customs regulations like TIR Convention and other transit regimes, particularly the criteria for access to ensure that only trustworthy operators benefit from the system, the criteria for access to the profession of transport operator, security requirements for road infrastructure management; and so on. This way, replication or reinvention of technical and administrative rules can be prevented and unnecessary expenses avoided.

Countries should set transparent insurance rules for all elements of the transport process that follow international standards. Countries should also introduce preferential conditions of visa delivery for professional drivers. Finally, they should strive for substantial transport security regulation, taking into account benefits and tools provided by existing international legal schemes of which they are or should become CPs.

Nurture effective institutional and implementation arrangements. The implementation of bilateral (and multilateral) agreements depends to a large extent on efficient institutional support. In particular, this concerns the decision-making process under the aegis of international instruments. Institutions like properly functioning joint committees (JCs) to govern the implementation of bilateral agreements should be set up. Attention should be paid to the transparency of decision making, meaning, in the first place, easy access for all interested parties to the text of agreements and the decisions of JCs.

A simple, efficient, and transparent transport permit management scheme should be operated from the moment of exchanging permits between CPs to the fair and open distribution of these permits among national haulers. CPs should take the responsibility for managing their agreement, including introduction into the agreement of clauses on amendments, the application of infringement procedures and related sanctions, and the application of tools of dispute settlement. CPs should also regularly exchange information on all legal and other domestic matters and changes that may have an impact on the implementation of bilateral agreements.

More attention should be paid to institution building and training of experts and officials engaged in the creation and administration of bilateral agreements on road freight transport. Training will help officials to apply the latest good practices from the international scene. The proper implementation of well-drafted international agreements should cover issues like transparency, efficient and fair permit management, and all matters related to the administration of agreements.

Reference major international obligations. Most countries are CPs to various international agreements whether bilateral or multilateral. They should, therefore, carefully consider the rights and obligations stemming from their international treaties when conceiving and implementing bilateral road transport agreements. Although bilateral agreements signed between separate pairs of countries cannot interfere with each other, they should respect multilateral obligations if both CPs are also parties to a multilateral convention that covers the same or similar issues. For example, the obligations of bilateral agreements may overlap with the World Trade Organization's General Agreement on Tariffs and Trade (GATT) and/or General Agreement on Trade in Services (GATS), with United Nations Economic Commission for Europe (UNECE) transport agreements, and so forth.

Furthermore, two CPs should duly take into account provisions of all relevant bilateral agreements they have concluded between themselves on issues that may be interrelated. For examples, the bilateral transport agreement of two CPs may be interrelated with a bilateral agreement on fiscal matters, or on customs checks at the CPs' frontiers. Governments should therefore conclude or amend and implement their bilateral road freight transport agreements with due respect to the general international legal context and all their international obligations.

Conclusion and Next Steps

This study makes it clear that a model is needed that could guide reforms and streamline the management of international relations in road freight transport. International road transport services are an extremely important part of international commerce, but they are currently regulated by a complex mix of bilateral instruments. It is clear that current practice is inefficient and likely increases costs of compliance. A well-considered model, offering options and expected outcomes, could greatly help to mould future bilateral agreements. Such a model could also help show where there are departures from international best practice. Obviously this was beyond the scope of the current study, but clearly it would be important to develop such a model. Future work in this area will be directed at identifying options and paths to road freight transport integration.

Specifically, further work will include the following actions:

- Expand the database of bilateral (and multilateral) road freight transport agreements to serve as a reference database for project design. The database can help countries deal effectively with one of the major costs in international trade.
- Articulate a practical implementation tool at the bilateral and multilateral levels, especially in low-income regions where transport costs are highest.
- Provide technical assistance on the domestic legal environment for bilateral road freight transport agreements.
- Assess in detail the economic importance of agreements (data collection, data simulation, detailed analysis).
- Estimate the quantifiable impact of various liberalization measures in road freight transport regulation on traffic, trade, and general national welfare levels.

Typology Questionnaire for Bilateral Road Freight Transport Agreements

A. Basic Data

1. Which are the two contracting parties to the agreement? Party A Party B
2. Name the continent where the contracting parties are located. Country A Country B
3. When was the agreement signed? Date: DD/MM/YYYY
4. When did the agreement enter into force? Date: DD/MM/YYYY
5. Does this agreement replace an older one? Yes _____ No _____ n.a. _____

If yes, does the agreement explicitly supersede the older version? If not, are there overlapping provisions? Which ones? (It is accepted that locating old agreements may not be easy).

6. Is the agreement reached under the umbrella of a wider framework agreement?

   Yes _____ No _____ n.a. _____

If yes, name the framework agreement

7. Is there a "definitions" chapter in the agreement? Yes ___ No ___

If yes, does it contain at least the important terms?

8. Are there provisions related to relationships with other treaties or prevalent law?

   (Reference to national law or bilateral agreement)

   Yes ___ No ___

   Which treaties/laws?

9. Has the agreement been concluded in the language(s) of the contracting parties and at least in one international language agreed by competent authorities of the contracting parties?

Language(s) of the contracting parties:

Also in one international language:

Which language copy is available for analysis?

10. Is the competent authority clearly nominated with full contact details? Yes ___ No ___

B. Coverage

11. Are there limitations in the geographical scope of the agreement? (For example, the CBTA agreement of the Greater Mekong Subregion or CAREC documents, where only one or two provinces of China are parties.)

    Yes ___ No ___

    If yes, specify.

12. Does the agreement provide for transport services between the parties to be exclusively performed by means of transport registered in one of the contracting parties?

    Yes ___ No ___

    If not, specify.

13. Does the agreement provide for transport services between the parties to be exclusively performed by transport operators duly authorized/licensed in one of the contracting parties?

    Yes ___ No ___

    If not, specify.

14. Are there types of transport that are totally prohibited?

    Yes ___No ___

    If yes, specify. Are the reasons included in the agreement?

15. List types of permits/authorizations applicable under the agreement for various operations allowed.

    Yes or No:

    _____ bilateral transport
    _____ transit transport
    _____ triangular (third-country) transport

_____ transport in border region (territory adjacent to national border between neighboring contracting parties)

_____ Other categories of permits, please explain:

16. Are there time limitations of less than one year for the use of issued transport permits?

Yes ___ No ___

If yes, specify.

17. Are there types of transport prohibited except with special authorization?

Yes ___ No ___

If yes, specify. (As for instance petroleum in article 7.6 of the Tanzania-Zambia agreement, attached in annex 4)

C. Permit/Authorization System

18. Is cabotage

- Completely prohibited
- Prohibited except under special authorization, and if so, specify the procedure and conditions of the authorization (Benchmark: ECMT/MA, articles 6.2 and 8.5)
- Allowed under certain conditions, if so, specify the procedures and conditions
- Allowed without restrictions

Specify procedures and conditions

19. Are there any types of traffic exempted from permit requirements?

Yes ___ No ___

20. If Yes to 14, what are the types of traffic exempted from permit requirements? (Benchmark: ECMT/MA article 7)

Yes or No

- Own account transport
- Transport of livestock
- Transport on an occasional basis, to or from airports, in cases where services are diverted
- Transport of vehicles which are damaged or have broken down and the transport of breakdown repair vehicles
- Unladen (empty) journey by a goods vehicle sent to replace a vehicle which has broken down in another country, and also the return journey, after repair, of the vehicle that had broken down

- Transport of spare parts and provisions for oceangoing ships and aircraft
- Transport of medical supplies and equipment needed for emergencies, more particularly in response to natural disasters and humanitarian needs
- Transport of works and objects of art for fairs and exhibitions or for non-commercial purposes
- Transport for noncommercial purposes of properties, accessories and animals to or from theatrical, musical, film, sports or circus performances (including race horses, race vehicles and boats), fairs or fetes, and those intended for radio recordings, or for film or television production
- Funeral transport
- Other category(ies) exempted from permit requirements, if yes, specify these categories below

21. Types of transport exempted from quota requirements

    (Benchmark: ECMT/MA Article 7.13)

    Yes or No

    - Removals
    - Perishable goods
    - Other category(ies) exempted from quota requirements, if yes specify definition(s) of the category(ies)

22. Are there provisions in the agreement related to

    Yes or No

    - Modalities for agreeing on the number of permits (annual quotas). Most common negotiations are carried on in the joint committee (JC), but it can also be done by correspondence between the competent authorities of the CPs.
    - Modalities and date of exchange of permits (by post, by diplomatic channels, and so forth). Normally the agreed number of permits should be exchanged at the end of the year, to ensure the necessary permit from the beginning of the coming year.
    - Conditions of validity. The permits for direct/bilateral transport are usually valid for one entry and a return journey, while the permits for transit transport to/from a third country are usually valid for one transit passage and return transit journey.
    - Conditions of use. Permit to be kept on the vehicles to which they belong, to be produced upon request to any person authorized in the territory of either country, not to be transferred between carriers, and so forth.
    - Any other important modalities?

23. Can permits be traded?

    Yes ___ No ___

24. Methodology of sharing the permits

    Yes or No
    - Is there a bilateral quota? This question is aimed at covering cases of bilaterals having completely liberalized traffic for example, some UK ones and Swiss ones. "Open-ended" is meant to cover cases where the quota is maintained formally but without quantitative limits.

    If Yes to previous question, is quota limit specified in the agreement?

    - If contained in the agreement, is there a sharing formula? Explain this formula below As a general rule, the formula is 50/50, but that is not the case, for instance, for many landlocked countries, where one can often see a 2/3, 1/3, or 60/40 split with the coastal state; hence the distinction below. One can also see instances where the trade-off is not between simple figures but involves more complex exchanges of the types described in the "IRU /UNECE questionnaire."
    - Are there additional quotas for vehicles meeting the most modern safety and emissions standards? (Benchmark: ECMT/MA, article 11.3.2)

    If yes, specify in the text box here-below.

    - Are there additional quotas rewarding the use of ROLA, RORO or the use of alternative routes?

    If yes, specify in the text box here-below.

    Specify quota sharing methods; quotas for modern vehicles and for intermodal transport

25. Existence, stipulated in the bilateral agreement of a "tour de rôle" (freight allocation/queuing) system as described for instance in Arvis, Raballand, and Marteau, 2010, "The Cost of being Landlocked," World Bank publication, page 19. (*Note:* if the "tour de rôle" stems from a national regulation tick the second box and describe succinctly the regulations, if available, and indicate its references.)

    Yes, bilateral tour de rôle
    No, unilateral tour de rôle
    No, no tour de rôle at all

    If yes, specify procedure, scope and modalities (bodies involved, price setting system, freight allocation system, and so forth)

26. Does the agreement provide for double approval procedure for permits (or individual applications for permit) by the two contracting parties? (As for instance in articles 8.5(ii) to 8.8 of the Tanzania-Zambia agreement)

    Yes ___ No ___

    If yes specify procedure and timing:

27. Is there a requirement for double approval for quotas by the two contracting parties?

Yes ___ No ___

If yes specify procedure and timing:

28. Are there specific rules on the different types of permits in terms of lengths of validity of permits (annual, monthly, temporary, other) and renewal procedures, that have not already been described above when detailing types of quotas and trips exchanged for bilateral, transit, and triangular quotas?

Yes ___ No ___

If yes, specify.

29. Are there limitations on the "depth" of operations allowed? (For example, maximum 70 kilometers from the border)

Yes ___ No ___

Specify definition of "adjacent border zones" if different from that of ECMT/MA article 7.1.13. Explain the type of permits to be used for this type of operations.

30. Are there requirements for permit issuance such as VAT certification, road worthiness certification, licensing, and ownership requirement?

Yes ___ No ___

If yes, specify.

D. Provisions on Transit

31. Does the agreement cover explicitly the transit through the territory of one contracting party by vehicles of the other contracting party to/from third countries, or only the bilateral transport?

Yes ___ No ___

32. Transit quotas

Yes or No

  – Transit is forbidden
  – Allowed in an open-ended manner
  – Allowed with limitations

If allowed with limitations, specify type of limitation valid for operators of both contracting parties (for example, of the types described in the IRU /UNECE questionnaire).

33. Are there additional transit quotas for vehicles meeting the most modern safety and emissions standards? (Benchmark: ECMT/MA, article 11.3.2)

Yes ___ No ___

If yes, specify.

34. Are there additional transit quotas rewarding the use of ROLA, RORO, or the use of alternative routes?

Yes ___ No ___

If yes, specify.

E. Triangular Quotas

35. Are triangular quotas present in the agreement? (If present with limitations please specify as indicated in the following questions.)

Open-ended; present with limitations; absent

36. Limitations of triangular operations:

Yes or No

– Special authorization required
– Existence of "self-transit obligation" (Benchmark: ECMT/MA, article 6.1.b)
– For the carriers of A from or to the territory B to or from the territory of a third party to the agreement "AB": number of round trips or monthly or annual quotas or other elements exchanged (for example, of the types described in the IRU/UNECE typology)
– For the carriers of B from or to the territory A to or from the territory of a third party to the agreement "AB": number of round trips or monthly or annual quotas or other elements exchanged (for example, of the types described in the IRU/UNECE typology

37. Are there additional triangular quotas for vehicles meeting the most modern safety and emissions standards? (Benchmark: ECMT/MA, article 11.3.2)

Yes ___ No ___

If yes, specify.

38. Are there additional triangular quotas rewarding the use of ROLA, RORO, or the use of alternative routes?

Yes ___ No ___

If yes, specify.

F. Prescribed Routes

39. Are there prescribed routes for transit or any other international operation?

    Yes ___ No ___

    If yes, specify the routes and the conditions if any:

40. Is the list of the designated routes included in the agreement or in an Annex thereto? (If further developments are to be considered and in order to make amendments easier, the list of the designated transit routes should be included in an Annex to the agreement.)

    Yes ___ No ___

41. If yes to previous question, are the following used as criteria for route specification?

    Yes or No

    - Status of infrastructure
    - Actual or potential volumes of transport/trade on those routes
    - Status of the border crossing points on the routes
    - Road capacity to process international transport in transit
    - Interest of the contracting party to promote the route

    Other, please specify:

42. Are there indications on the technical parameters/design standards of the designated routes? (Logically, these parameters should comply with those of the regional transport infrastructure networks in order to ensure interconnectivity and interoperability.)

    Yes ___ No ___

43. Is there a statement/commitment/decision of the contracting parties to make, whenever possible, the following facilities available for traffic in transit (or any other international operation) along the designated roads, against payment, to the rates that apply to the nationals of the country in which the facilities are used:

    Yes or No

    - First aid services and other assistance in case of accidents
    - Repair facilities in case of breakdown of vehicles
    - Fuel filling stations
    - Post and telecommunication offices
    - Facilities for loading, unloading, break bulk
    - Storage areas and building
    - Restaurants and stopover rest facilities
    - Secure truck parking areas

44. Are prescribed exit/entry points for transit or any other international operations specified in the agreement? (As for instance in article 4.1.d of the Tanzania-Zambia agreement)

Yes ___ No ___

G. Fiscal Measures

45. Are vehicles from the other contracting party exempted from taxes relating to ownership, registration, running of the vehicle, and special taxes on transport services?

(Benchmark: ECMT/MA article 9.1)

Yes ___ No ___ Partially ____

If no or if partially, specify:

46. Specify if the agreement contains a definition of "taxes related to the running of the vehicle" and/or of "special taxes on transport services."

47. Are fuel contained in built-in tankers, lubricants, and spare parts exempted of all import duties? (Benchmark: ECMT/MA article 9.2)

Yes ___ No ___

If not, specify.

48. Are the initial and terminal legs of combined transport exempted from tolls and duties? (Benchmark: ECMT/MA article 9.3)

Yes ___ No ___

49. Are other types of traffic totally or partially exempted from tolls and duties?

Yes ___ No ___

If yes, specify.

H. Vehicles and Drivers

50. Does the agreement contain technical requirements for vehicles?

Yes ___ No ___

51. Are there specific provisions on weight and dimensions included in the bilateral agreement?

Yes ___ No ___

52. Are there provisions related to the mutual recognition of weighing certificates of vehicles? (See United Nations International Convention on the Harmonization of Frontier Controls of Goods ["Harmonization Convention"], 1982)

    Yes ___ No ___

53. Are there provisions related to the mutual recognition of technical inspection certificates? (See "Harmonization Convention.")

    Yes ___ No ___

54. Can a vehicle in combination be made up of vehicle units registered in different countries?

    Yes ___ No ___

If yes, specify.

55. Are there provisions related to the mutual recognition of driving licenses?

    Yes ___ No ___

If yes, are there provisions related to the format and content of the driving license?

56. Are there provisions related to mandatory (maximum) driving and (minimum) rest periods for the drivers performing transport operations under the agreement?

    Yes ___ No ___

If yes, specify.

57. Are there requirements of certificates proving special qualifications of the driver? (for example, in case of transport of dangerous goods)

    Yes ___ No ___

If yes, specify.

I. Transport Operator

58. Are there provisions related to compulsory motor vehicle third-party insurance?

    Yes ___ No ___

If yes, specify.

59. Are there provisions related to the liability of the carrier?

    Yes ___ No ___

If yes, specify.

60. Does the agreement give the carrier the right to establish offices and/or appoint representatives and/or agencies in the territory of the other contracting party?

    Yes ___ No ___

If yes, specify.

J. Specific Facilitation and Other Matters

61. Is nondiscriminatory treatment (of goods, vehicle, and driver) clearly stated as an obligation in the agreement?

    Yes ____ No ____ Partially ____

If yes or partially, specify.

62. Are there provisions explicitly related to environment protection?

    Yes ___ No ___

If yes, specify.

63. Are there provisions explicitly related to safety (traffic and/or transport operation)?

    Yes ___ No ___

If yes, specify.

64. Are there provisions explicitly related to security (traffic and/or transport operation)?

    Yes ___ No ___

If yes, specify.

65. Are there provisions on preferential facilitation measures for the driver (simplified immigration formalities such as passport/visa, driving licenses, and so forth), vehicles (registration, road worthiness, weights and dimensions, insurance), and goods (customs, quality, phytosanitary, veterinary checks), special expeditious treatment in case of transports of special cargoes (dangerous goods, livestock and perishable goods, temporary admission of certain goods and means of transport)?

    Yes ___ No ___

If yes, specify.

66. Shall any other transport document than permits /authorizations be carried on board the vehicles to be presented if requested? (For example, a consignment note)

    Yes ___ No ___

If yes, specify.

K. Implementation Arrangements

67. Joint Committee:

Yes ___ No ___

– Are the provisions regarding the JC different or more specific than those contained in article 14 of the ECMT/MA? (For example, composition, meeting periodicity, automatic allocation of quotas if no meeting within a certain duration, and so forth)
– Are decisions of the JC to be made public?

Specify JC institutional mechanism and the way of publishing JC decisions.

68. Are there procedures in case of infringement of agreement provisions?

Most bilateral agreements allow the authorities of host countries to take action on infringement of rules in their territories with notice to the competent authorities of home countries. Some agreements also provide for details of the sanctions for infringement, such as warning, temporary suspension or cancellation of the permit. Having the procedures included in the agreement avoids disputes between the contracting parties and lengthy debates in the meetings of the JC.

Yes ___ No ___

If yes, specify.

69. Is exchange of information an obligation under the agreement?

Yes ___ No ___

If yes, on which subjects? (for example, on infringements, sanctions, national rules and regulations, new national practices, and so forth)

L. Agreement Final Provisions

70. Are there provisions related to:

Yes ___ No ___

– Registration of the agreement with the Secretary General of the United Nations (according to the Charter of the United Nations, Chapter XVI, Miscellaneous Provisions, Article 102)
– Transparency and availability of pieces of national legislation and regulations
– Right of appeal against decisions of competent authorities

- Dispute settlement arrangements
- Procedures of amendment of the agreement including its Annexes and/or Protocols
- Is there a provision to consult the other party when reviewing regulations relating to the agreement?
- Entry into force and duration (clause of automatic extension?)
- Authentic text (one, two or more languages)

Specific Bilateral Road Freight Transport Agreements Selected for Benchmarking

	Geographic relation	Contracting parties	Language version
1.	**Europe-Europe**	Belarus-Belgium	English
2.		Belarus-Denmark	English
3.		Belarus-Netherlands	English
4.		Belarus-Switzerland	German
5.		Bosnia and Herzegovina-Switzerland	German
6.		Czech Republic-Turkey	English
7.		Finland-Albania	English
8.		Macedonia, FYR-Spain	English
9.		Macedonia, FYR-Switzerland	German
10.		Macedonia, FYR-United Kingdom	English
11.		Serbia-Luxembourg	French
12.		Serbia-Spain	English
13.		Serbia-Switzerland	German
14.		Serbia-United Kingdom	English
15.		Bulgaria-Turkey	English
16.		Turkey-France	English
17.		Ukraine-France	English
18.		Switzerland-Albania	German
1.	**Asia-Europe**	Afghanistan-France	English
2.		Austria-Iran, Islamic Rep.	English
3.		Iran, Islamic Rep.-Belgium	English
4.		Iran, Islamic Rep.-Finland	English
5.		Iran, Islamic Rep.-Germany	German
6.		Iran, Islamic Rep.-Spain	Spanish
7.		Iran, Islamic Rep.-Turkey	English
8.		Israel-Belgium	English
9.		Israel-France	English
10.		Jordan-Switzerland	German
11.		Jordan-United Kingdom	English
12.		Kazakhstan-Hungary	Russian
13.		Kazakhstan-Lithuania	Russian
14.		Kazakhstan-Moldova	Russian

(*table continues on next page*)

	Geographic relation	Contracting parties	Language version
15.		Kazakhstan-Netherlands	Russian
16.		Kazakhstan-Poland	Russian
17.		Kazakhstan-Romania	Russian
18.		Kazakhstan-Slovak Republic	Russian
19.		Kazakhstan-Spain	Russian
20.		Kazakhstan-Sweden	Russian
21.		Kazakhstan-Switzerland	German
22.		Kazakhstan-United Kingdom	English
23.		Switzerland-Azerbaijan	German
24.		Switzerland-Georgia	German
25.		Switzerland-Syrian Arab Republic	German
26.		Syrian Arab Republic-Finland	English
27.		Syrian Arab Republic-Sweden	English
28.		Uzbekistan-Germany	German
29.		Uzbekistan-Netherlands	English
1.	**Africa-Europe**	Algeria-Spain	Spanish
2.		Algeria-Switzerland	German
3.		Morocco-Finland	English
4.		Morocco-Luxembourg/Belgium	French
5.		Morocco-Spain	English
6.		Morocco-Switzerland	German
7.		Morocco-United Kingdom	English
8.		Tunisia-Austria	French
9.		Tunisia-Finland	English
10.		Tunisia-France	English
11.		Tunisia-Spain	French
12.		Tunisia-Switzerland	German
13.		Tunisia-United Kingdom	English
1.	**Asia-Asia**	Kazakhstan-Jordan	Russian
2.		Kazakhstan-Kyrgyzstan	Russian
3.		Kazakhstan-Mongolia	Russian
4.		Kazakhstan-Pakistan	Russian
5.		Kazakhstan-Tajikistan	Russian
6.		Kazakhstan-Turkmenistan	Russian
7.		Kazakhstan-Uzbekistan	Russian
8.		Lao PDR-Vietnam	English
9.		Lebanon-Syrian Arab Republic	English
1.	**Africa-Africa**	Mozambique-South Africa	English
2.		South Africa-Zambia	English
3.		South Africa-Zimbabwe	English
4.		South Africa-Malawi	English
5.		Tanzania-Zambia	English
6.		Cameroon-Chad	French
7.		Cameroon-Central African Republic	French
1.	**South America**	Brazil-Venezuela, RB	English

Source: World Bank.

Economic Importance Positions of Agreements by Trade and Vehicle Fleet Size

Agreement	Fleet size 2008	Trade volume	Score
Algeria-Spain	5,680,585	12,285,105	41
Algeria-Switzerland	601,232	588,798	36
Austria-Iran, Islamic Rep.	681,338	547,433	45
Bosnia and Herzegovina-Switzerland	383,453	199,141	65
Bulgaria-Turkey	3,109,385	3,159,134	72
Finland-Albania	466,733	12,335	36
Iran, Islamic Rep.-Belgium	962,780	198,921	42
Iran, Islamic Rep.-Finland	678,475	202,690	68
Iran, Islamic Rep.-Germany	4,546,299	6,084,030	75
Iran, Islamic Rep.-Spain	5,705,585	541,841	47
Iran, Islamic Rep.-Turkey	3,110,224	1,282,600	35
Israel-Belgium	1,021,453	7,931,420	61
Israel-France	6,638,673	3,251,514	35
Kazakhstan-Hungary	842,066	526,871	53
Kazakhstan-Lithuania	564,440	330,528	52
Kazakhstan-Moldova	530,299	260,352	54
Kazakhstan-Netherlands	1,485,764	5,137,125	51
Kazakhstan-Poland	3,124,029	900,528	44
Kazakhstan-Romania	1,059,672	1,092,728	73
Kazakhstan-Slovak Republic	661,225	835,142	53
Kazakhstan-Spain	5,819,917	990,642	55
Kazakhstan-Sweden	922,997	678,504	38
Kazakhstan-Switzerland	740,564	11,448,790	38
Kazakhstan-Turkmenistan	518,582	222,898	62
Kazakhstan-United Kingdom	4,169,032	2,196,936	73
Macedonia, FYR-Spain	5,434,465	113,799	62
Macedonia, FYR-Switzerland	355,112	78,508	32
Macedonia, FYR-United Kingdom	3,783,580	108,783	74
Morocco-Finland	448,303	315,707	32
Morocco-Luxembourg	104,247	22,793	36
Morocco-Spain	5,475,413	9,039,019	36
Morocco-Switzerland	396,060	623,508	37
Morocco-United Kingdom	3,824,528	1,589,401	43

(table continues on next page)

Agreement	Fleet size 2008	Trade volume	Score
Serbia-Luxembourg	205,306	8,964	43
Serbia-Spain	5,576,472	297,291	39
Serbia-Switzerland	497,119	337,362	45
Serbia-United Kingdom	3,925,587	380,979	44
South Africa-Zimbabwe	134,675	2,400,218	27
Switzerland-Albania	414,490	39,622	71
Switzerland-Azerbaijan	430,372	129,912	58
Switzerland-Georgia	380,632	31,239	58
Tunisia-Austria	551,338	122,918	28
Tunisia-Finland	548,475	88,348	49
Tunisia-France	6,450,000	10,366,238	36
Tunisia-Spain	5,575,585	1,966,050	46
Tunisia-Switzerland	496,232	589,364	35
Tunisia-United Kingdom	3,924,700	1,299,517	39
Turkey-France	9,090,224	15,023,701	28
Ukraine-France	6,731,106	2,173,895	43

Source: World Bank.

BIBLIOGRAPHY

Armstrong, M., and D. E. M. Sappington. 2006. "Regulation, Competition, and Liberalization." *Journal of Economic Literature* 44 (2): 325–66.

Arvis, J. F., G. Raballand, and J. F. Marteau. 2010. *The Cost of Being Landlocked: Logistics Costs and Supply Chain Reliability.* Washington, DC: World Bank.

Bernadet, M. 2009. "The Construction and Operation of the Road Freight Transport Market in Europe." Forum Paper 2009–1, International Transport Forum, Paris.

Borchert, I., B. Gootiiz, and A. Mattoo. 2010. "Trade Policy Restrictiveness in Transportation." Presentation at OECD Expert Meeting on Transport Services, World Bank, Washington, DC, November.

Carbajo, J. 1993. *Regulatory Reform in Transport: Some Recent Experiences.* Washington, DC: World Bank.

Chemonics International. 2011. "Study on Impact of Transportation Monopoly: Report on the Roads Goods Transport Industry of Nepal." U.S. Agency for International Development (USAID), Kathmandu.

Dutz, M., A. Hayri, and P. Ibarra. 2000. "Regulatory Reform, Competition and Innovation: A Case Study of the Mexican Road Freight Industry." Policy Research Working Paper 2318, World Bank, Washington, DC.

ECMT (European Conference of Ministers of Transport). 1997. "Recommendation Framework for Bilateral Agreements in Road Transport [CEMT/CM(97) 21–CM(97)21/ADD1]." ECMT, Paris.

———. 2001. "Regulatory Reform in Road Freight Transport Proceedings of the International Seminar." ECMT, Paris, February.

Gray, R., N. A. Fattah, and S. Cullinane. 1998. "Road Freight Privatization in Egypt: Is Big Beautiful?" *Journal of Transport Geography* 6: 33–41.

IRU (International Road Transport Union). 2009. "Road Transport in the People's Republic of China." IRU, Geneva. http://www.iru.org/en_bookshop_item?id=2.

ITF (International Transport Forum). 2009. "ECMT Multilateral Quota User Guide." ITF in cooperation with the International Road Transport Union (IRU), ITF, Paris.

———. 2011. "Report of the High Level Group for the Development of the Multilateral Quota System." ITF(2011)3, ITF, Paris.

Law, D., and M. Versteeg. 2012. "The Declining Influence of the United States Constitution." *New York University Law Review* 87: 1–86.

Maasdorp, G. 2001. *Liberalisation of Transport Services in SADC and at the Multilateral Level.* London: Commonwealth Secretariat.

Mwase, N. 2003. "The Liberalization, De-regulation, and Privatization of the Transport Sector in Sub-Saharan Africa: Experiences, Challenges and Opportunities." *Journal of African Economies* 12: 153–92.

Nick Poree Associates. 2010. "Facilitation of Road Transport Market Liberalisation in the SADC Region, Final Report." Southern African Development Community (SADC), Gaborone.

OECD (Organisation for Economic Co-operation and Development). 2010. *Globalisation, Transport and the Environment*. Paris: OECD.

Raballand, G., C. Kunaka, and B. Giersing. 2008. "The Impact of Regional Liberalization and Harmonization in Road Transport Services: A Focus on Zambia and Lessons for Landlocked Countries." Policy Research Working Paper 4482, World Bank, Washington, DC.

Raballand, G., and P. Macchi. 2008. "Transport Prices and Costs: The Need to Revisit Donors' Policies in Transport in Africa." Working Paper No. 190, Bureau for Research and Economic Analysis of Development (BREAD), Washington, DC.

SADC (Southern African Development Community). 1996. "SADC Protocol on Transport, Communications and Meteorology." Southern African Transport Communications Commission (SATCC), Maputo.

Scheerlink, I., L. Hens, and R. S'Jegers. 1998. "On the Road to Transport Liberalization: Belgian Road Haulers Policy Preferences." *Journal of Transport Economics and Policy* 32 (3):365–76.

Teravaninthorn, S., and G. Raballand. 2009. *Transport Prices and Costs in Africa: A Review of the Main International Corridors*. Washington, DC: World Bank.

Togan, S. 2009. "Liberalization of Transport Services in Egypt, Jordan and Morocco." Policy Research Paper No. 31, Economic Research Forum (ERF), Cairo.

UNESCAP (United Nations Economic and Social Commission for Asia and the Pacific). 2007. "Towards Harmonized Legal Regime on Transport Facilitation in the ESCAP Region—Guidelines." ST/ESCAP/2489, UNESCAP, New York.

U.S. Chamber of Commerce. 2006. *Land Transport Options between Europe and Asia: Commercial Feasibility Study*. Washington, DC: U.S. Chamber of Commerce.

Ward, N., and E. Baretto. 2011. "Technical Report: Road Freight Transport Services Diagnostic Study." USAID Southern Africa TradeHub, Gaborone.

World Bank. 1996. *Sustainable Transport Priorities for Policy Sector Reform*. Washington, DC: World Bank.

———. 2011. "Infrastructure and Trade Facilitation in Sub-Saharan Africa: An Agenda for Reform." Submission to G20, World Bank, Washington, DC.

———. 2012. *Eurasia Cities: New Realities Along the Silk Road*. Washington, DC: World Bank.

WTO (World Trade Organization). 2006. "Quantitative Air Services Agreements Review (QUASAR)." WTO S/C/W/270/Add.1-3, WTO, Geneva.

———. 2010. "Road Freight Transport Services: Background Note by the Secretariat." S/C/W/324, WTO, Geneva.

ECO-AUDIT
Environmental Benefits Statement

The World Bank is committed to preserving endangered forests and natural resources. The Office of the Publisher has chosen to print World Bank Studies and Working Papers on recycled paper with 30 percent postconsumer fiber in accordance with the recommended standards for paper usage set by the Green Press Initiative, a non-profit program supporting publishers in using fiber that is not sourced from endangered forests. For more information, visit www.greenpressinitiative.org.

In 2010, the printing of this book on recycled paper saved the following:
- 11 trees*
- 3 million Btu of total energy
- 1,045 lb. of net greenhouse gases
- 5,035 gal. of waste water
- 306 lb. of solid waste

* 40 feet in height and 6–8 inches in diameter

green
press
INITIATIVE